It Happened to Me

Series Editor: Arlene Hirschfelder

Books in the "It Happened to Me" series are designed for inquisitive teens digging for answers about certain illnesses, social issues, or lifestyle interests. Whether you are deep into your teen years or just entering them, these books are gold mines of up-to-date information, riveting teen views, and great visuals to help you figure out stuff. Besides special boxes highlighting singular facts, each book is enhanced with the latest reading list, websites, and an index. Perfect for browsing, there's loads of expert information by acclaimed writers to help parents, guardians, and librarians understand teen illness, tough situations, and lifestyle choices.

1. *Learning Disabilities: The Ultimate Teen Guide,* by Penny Hutchins Paquette and Cheryl Gerson Tuttle, 2002.
2. *Epilepsy: The Ultimate Teen Guide,* by Kathlyn Gay and Sean McGarrahan, 2002.
3. *Stress Relief: The Ultimate Teen Guide,* by Mark Powell, 2002.

STRESS RELIEF

The Ultimate Teen Guide

MARK POWELL

Illustrations by Kelly Adams

It Happened to Me, No. 3

The Scarecrow Press, Inc.
Lanham, Maryland • Toronto • Plymouth, UK

SCARECROW PRESS, INC.

Published in the United States of America
by Scarecrow Press, Inc.
A wholly owned subsidary of
The Rowman & Littlefield Publishing Group, Inc.
4501 Forbes Boulevard, Suite 200, Lanham, Maryland 20706
www.scarecrowpress.com

Estover Road
Plymouth PL6 7PY
United Kingdom

Copyright © 2002 by Mark Powell
First paperback edition 2007

British Library Cataloguing in Publication Information Available

The hardback edition of this book was previously cataloged by the Library of Congress
as follows:
Powell, Mark, 1963–
    Stress relief : the ultimate teen guide / Mark Powell ; illustrations by Kelly Adams.
        p. cm.—(It happened to me ; no. 3)
Summary: Describes the causes of stress, how to recognize and deal with them, and
how to alleviate the stress itself by using such methods as breathing exercises,
meditation, and creative visualization.
Includes bibliographical references and index.
    ISBN 0-8108-4433-8 (alk. paper)
  1. Stress in adolescence—Juvenile literature. 2. Stress management for teenagers—
Juvenile literature. [1. Stress (Psychology) 2. Anxiety.] I. Adams, Kelly, ill. II. Title.
III. Series.
    BF724.3.S86 P69 2002
    155.5'18—dc21   2002007227

ISBN: 0-8108-4433-8 (hardcover)
ISBN: 978-0-8108-5806-0 / 0-8108-5806-1 (paperback)

Contents

RADIANT INNER PEACE:

A Teenager's Guide to Totally Transforming Stress and Anything Like It

Contents

Introduction

The problem with most of the ten zillion "stress reduction" books out there is that all the techniques they dole out just feel like more things to add to our already depressing "to-do" list; "I'm already feeling overwhelmed and now I'm supposed to add meditation and deep breathing and Lord knows what all else to my crazy schedule?" Plus, most of them offer symptomatic relief—ways to relax once we're already stressed-out—but what about the cause of stress in the first place?

There are also approaches out there that teach us about the root cause of our stress—how we think about ourselves and life—but these approaches take a while to really learn about. In the meantime we also need some things we can do RIGHT NOW to feel more relaxed and at ease.

This book combines the best of both. It provides a bucket to quickly scoop out enough water to immediately "stop your boat from sinking" AND it provides you with the stuff to patch the hole in the boat so no more "water" comes in.

What's more, this book is very "user friendly": I won't be just dumping an intimidating list of "stress management techniques" on your lawn and driving away. I'll be teaching you in a natural, organized way, from the most essential, bottom-line approaches to the more peripheral ones. You can imagine them in concentric circles, like a bull's-eye. At the very dead center is what some people call "stress prevention." This is the bottom line, the real deal; plugging the hole in the boat. It has to do with attending to our thinking, our core beliefs, who we think we are in the world.

The rest of the circles surrounding the center are all things to do and work on *once the stress has already gotten*

I won't be just dumping an intimidating list of "stress management" techniques on your lawn and driving away. I'll be teaching you in a natural, organized way . . .

into you and started making you feel uptight. They move out from the center in order of importance. For example, the very first ring out includes the very most important things for getting rid of stress. The basics. Then, if you want to do more to wash away your stress you can "move out a ring" and play around with some methods that are a little less central, and so on. It's entirely up to you and how badly you want to feel really good. You take it as far as you like. My hope, of course, is that you'll get into the process so much that, at some point, you'll find yourself totally, happily committed to the most rare and wonderful depths of serenity possible, what I'm calling radiant inner peace.

The last thing before we get started is this: This is a book on stress management and stress reduction, but

I just happen to HATE the terms "stress management" and "stress reduction." What bleak terms! They're bleak because they're stated totally negatively.

They're only terms about what we don't want. They give no image or picture of what we do want. That's not how anyone creates anything. Imagine Renoir standing before his blank, white canvas, vividly visualizing what he doesn't want to paint. Imagine him calling his painting "whiteness reduction." We need clear, positive ideas, pictures, ideals to focus on and to move toward.

So instead of "stress management" or "stress reduction," begin right now to

think in terms of what you do want instead. A feeling of deep ease and relaxation at the core of your being. A feeling of looseness, playfulness. The constant sense of a rich abundance of time, every day. The experience of spacious openness. An easy trust of life; a calm and inner stillness. A quiet mind and a peaceful heart. Think in these terms.

These are the kinds of things I mean when I speak of Radiant Inner Peace. But make up your own. Maybe for you it's not words, but a feeling. The point is, know the direction you're moving in, at whatever pace is right for you. This is a very good place to start.

The Problem

WHAT IS STRESS?

These days pretty much everyone knows what stress is. We know it way too well. It's that feeling of tension, of strain, of being under pressure. It's that anxious feeling of "running scared." Maybe we feel "stressed-out" because of some huge, gruesome math test, or maybe because our boyfriend or girlfriend is leaving us to join a UFO worshipping cult in Ohio, but we all get stressed-out, and we all know what it feels like.

By the way, in this book when we use the word "stress," we're using it in the casual, nontechnical sense; the way regular people use the word, not the way biologists use it. When scientist types—physiologists, biologists and those folks—talk about stress they usually mean "any stimulus which elicits any physiological response from the organism" (that's you). So technically, eating an innocent looking grape "stresses" the system, inasmuch as the body now has to do stuff to process that grape. Even happy things, like winning a gold medal in the Olympics, create this sort of "stress" because they create all sorts of happiness hormones and adrenaline and general "physiological arousal." Some authors have called this "good stress."

The stress from grapes and gold medals is NOT the stress we're talking about in this book. We're talking about that nasty old emotional stress that we all know and hate. The kind that stops us from smiling and laughing as much as we'd like; the kind where our breathing is thin and shallow and we're tired a lot and we don't think as clearly

SELYE ON STRESS

The term "stress" as it is popularly used today (as in "I'm feeling stressed-out") was made popular by a guy named Dr. Hans Selye in the 1920s. Dr. Selye was building on the work of a Harvard physiologist named Dr. Walter Cannon. Dr. Selye did tons of famous research showing how the common thread among nearly all sick people was a fundamental stress reaction in the body. If this stress reaction in the body—associated with all sorts of stress hormones shooting around—is prolonged over time, the results—in terms of physical and mental illness—were not pretty. In other words, over time, stress damages the body in numerous grisly ways.

Another thing Dr. Selye proved is that this stress response in the body is the same no matter what the ostensible cause of the stress (cold, heat, infection, trauma, fear, sexy vamp girl in your boyfriend's math class flirting with him, etc.).

because our thoughts are a racing jumble. When we're feeling emotionally stressed we're distracted, unable to pay much real attention to the people we're with and we snap at them. We lose and forget things. Our muscles are held tensely, around the jaw, the stomach, the shoulders and neck, the low back. Sometimes we chew on our lips, hair, fingernails, or anything else we can get into our mouth. We tap our foot nervously or bounce our knee up and down unconsciously. We always feel rushed and time seems to zoom along at a bewildering pace. We notice much less around us; our peripheral field of vision actually shrinks.

What a depressing list! The funny thing is how often people think that stress is some sort of special, mysterious bit of voodoo, like a flu bug or something, but truly, what we call

"stress" is nothing but plain old emotions, mostly fear but usually with some anger thrown in for good measure.

Most often we feel the fear first, then we unconsciously react to the fear with anger and we shove both the fear and the anger way down inside us and the tense, agitated discomfort that's left over we call "stress." But enough on what stress is. Let's take a look at what causes stress.

WHAT CAUSES STRESS?

What causes stress, plain and simple, is our thinking. But this is an awfully radical thought and we'll have a lot to say about it later. As a matter of fact, the entire second part of this entire book is about this. For now, let's pretend that "things out there" "cause" stress, and look at the sort of "conventional" inventory of these "causes," the kind of list more traditional, ordinary "stress reduction books" are chock full of. Here it is.

- ◯ **Big change. The death of a loved one. Moving. A new job. Earth destroyed by moody aliens in flying saucers. All of that sort of thing. El majoro stresso.**

- ◯ **Gnarly, unsupportive, dysfunctional people. Toxic people. Mean people. Subtly mean people. Not subtly mean people. People who don't wish the very best for us. People who think we need to change or improve ourselves. Negative people. Abusive people. People who make us feel crazy, yucky, inadequate, or like we need a bath. Or like they need a bath.**

DID YOU KNOW?

In the 1950s, cardiologists Thomas Holmes and Richard Rahe explored the link between life changes and stress. They did this by surveying 7,000 people. Holmes and Rahe defined stress as the amount of adjustment needed to deal with a life change. They came up with a list (the "stress scale") of the top 43 most stressful life changes. It's a fairly famous list, and is frequently referred to in other books on stress. Holmes and Rahe showed that people with "higher scores" (more and bigger life changes) were the most likely to get an illness.

Topping the list as "most stressful life changes" are the death of a spouse, marital separation, and the death of a family member. Positive life changes are stressful too, by Holmes' and Rahe's definition, because they also require adjustments. For example, if you suddenly became ruler of the world, you might have to hire a secretary and buy some new, regal outfits. Very stressful.

○ **Life pressures and obligations. From school, from coaches, from jobs, from teams we're on, from theater casts we're part of, from parents and their not-always-wise expectations.**

People also report feeling intensely stressed-out by "the little things" too. Insane drivers, unmoving lines at the bank when you're already late for an important date, videotapes being eaten by VCRs, losing things, disgruntled cats peeing on your clothes, yucky headlines in the paper. All of that kind of thing.

Probably the most commonplace source of stress for people, on a day-to-day level, is simply the experience of having too much to do in not enough time. Deadlines. Obligations. Time shortages. Feeling overwhelmed. Feeling like the pace of your day is just way too fast; out of control even.

All of these are very real causes of stress, and we'll look at them and others and we'll talk about what to do about them. But one of the major premises of this book is that, at the deepest level,

the experience of feeling stressed comes from within our own head, our own habitual ways of seeing and thinking about our day and our life and ourselves.

STRESS:

- ▶ **damages relationships.**
- ▶ **makes us moody.**
- ▶ **makes us lousy listeners.**
- ▶ **zaps our energy.**
- ▶ **makes us tense.**
- ▶ **cheats us from enjoying life.**

Stress doesn't "come at us" from "out there;" it doesn't "happen to us;" "life" or "the world" does not stress us out. We do. At first this may seem like an annoying suggestion, but we hope that by the time you've finished reading this book, you'll see that this is the very best, very happiest news you could possibly hear about stress, because it means the power to change it lies not "out there" in circumstances, but within you, and you alone.

THE RESULTS OF STRESS

The results of stress are not pretty. In the "What Is Stress?" segment I spoke a bit about the immediate effects of stress, the ones we feel right now, in the moment. You'd think that "just" ruining your happiness on a day-to-day basis would be enough of a price to pay for our stress. Ah, but it's not! It gets worse. Quite ugly.

First of all, by wreaking havoc on our happiness, it very profoundly damages our relationships. Put more bluntly, it tends to ruin them. When we are stressed-out, we are not present with our friends. We're self-absorbed, closed, and unrelational, maybe even moody. We're really lousy listeners. We have no free energy and attention available for our friends. We snap and snarl at them. We are no fun. We make them tense just by our agitated presence. We cheat them from receiving the beauty of our spirit that shines out when we are at ease.

STRESS:
- is painful.
- destroys our creative abilities.
- is devastating to our health.

In other words, there are astounding gifts in each of us; these gifts could be just the trick, to truly help our friends, to really serve our families, to create all kinds of ripples of groovy vibrations that could be spreading out all over the place. But by being stressed-out we never let these gifts out to see the light of day. Incidentally, it's also just plain painful for the people who love us to see us all tense and miserable. So our stress-pain isn't just rotten for us; it hurts others too. It's good to pry our attention off ourselves long enough to notice this, because it can help motivate us to change our lives.

Secondly, stress destroys our ability to create what we want to create in our lives. You name it: good grades, an amazing rap band, masterful writing, excellence in dance or painting, or just a really cool party. The stressed-out person has severe handicaps in creating any such things. He is an unfocused, distracted person, one who is moody and fitful rather than even and steady; ineffective, inconsistent, scattered, not wholehearted, clear and focused. Also, really creative juice and inspiration requires some looseness, some bigness of spirit; stress makes us hard, contracted and creatively dried up.

Third, and this one's a biggie, stress is devastating to our bodily health. There are countless books on this subject and many tons of research too, but for now you should at least be aware that there's a very huge and very depressing list of health problems caused by our old friend, emotional stress. This list includes everything from headaches to back pain (and other musculoskeletal pains) to all sorts of digestive problems to a degraded immune system. And on and on. Basically, think of the most nasty, gruesome disease you can. Stress either causes it, makes it way worse, or makes recovering from it much more difficult and unlikely. Or all three. No joke.

A FEW SOBERING FACTS ABOUT STRESS

▶ Between 80 and 90 percent of all illness is stress-related. (Other researchers believe that all illness—at least in part—is stress-related.)
▶ Nearly 100 million Americans suffer from stress-related illness.
▶ Between 75 and 90 percent of all visits to the doctor are for stress and anxiety-related concerns.
▶ Stress is linked to the six leading causes of death— heart disease, cancer, lung disease, accidents, cirrhosis of the liver and suicide.

Excerpt from Lori Leyden-Rubenstein, *The Stress Management Handbook*. New Canaan, Conn.: Keats Publishing, 1998.

STRESS AND OUR SOCIETY (OR, YOU'D HAVE TO BE CRAZY NOT TO FEEL CRAZY IN OUR CULTURE)

Most people breathe a little sigh of relief when they discover that our culture is stark raving mad when it comes to stress and doing too much. Because it makes it much more understandable (almost unavoidable) that we're stressed-out. As a society, we reward compulsive workaholics, we praise frenetic busyness. We use words like "dynamic" and "motivated" to describe people who are driving themselves to a nervous breakdown.

In the United States, we have what's called a "Puritan work ethic." In common talk, that means that things like pleasure, enjoying leisure, celebrations, recreation, fun and relationships don't count, don't matter and are even somehow bad. "Idle hands are the devil's workshop" and all of that rot. What is good and admirable is work, hard labor, and plenty of it. Not just to provide for yourself and your loved ones, but just to work for work's sake; to deny yourself pleasure and enjoyment.

Most people of the world view this as patent, certifiable insanity, plain and simple. In most European countries, for example, the most value is put not on "accomplishing" a zillion "tasks" but on enjoying friends and family; good leisurely discussion; slow, pleasurable meals with people; love and art, music, literature. The value is put on living, and work is just one small slice of that pie. Their entire pace is different; their worldview is different. To them, what is the point of working grimly and miserably all the way through your life only to die and be buried? That's what worker ants and bees do. The point of life is to enjoy it fully with all your dear friends and to die with a heart full of rich, deep, vibrant memories and experiences. But in our society, "too much" enjoyment, pleasure and relaxation are looked at suspiciously; we're supposed to feel guilt for such things! In our society, the sure way to get approval from people is to tell them how incredibly busy we are, how we're juggling ten projects and are hot in pursuit of our lofty goals.

Certainly one way that this peculiarly American madness shows itself is in our societal pace; the "speed" and "rhythm" at which we live our lives; the way we look at, and live within, time.

In older times, and even today in many indigenous cultures, life was based upon natural, regular rhythms. Sunrise and sunset largely shaped our day; the workday was usually over when the sun set. The seasons and agricultural cycles shaped our months. Rhythms like these connected us to the earth, to our living, organic environment and to each other. These cyclic rhythms lived in our bodies, creating a deep feeling of order, regularity, and balance. There was no point in getting frantic. The crops were going to require harvesting around the same time anyway, and so on.

Now, in our modern age, very little of our lifestyle is shaped by anything even remotely organic or natural. Our schedules have almost nothing to do with the earth, with our bodies or with any sane, measured rhythms. Rather, electrical, artificial devices—clocks, computers, palm pilots,

HEALTH: JUST ONE FINE REASON TO WORK TOWARD RADIANT INNER PEACE

"There is considerable evidence . . . that the psychological effects of urgency—stress, anxiety, tension—do not stay in the psyche. They are translated into the body where they eventuate in physical ailments. The sense of urgency generates infirmity, disease, and death.

"In contrast, the psychological sense that accompanies the perception of time as static and non-flowing is one of tranquility, serenity and peace. This is the time perception so well described in mystical and poetic literature. It is the sense of oneness, of unity with all there is, the feeling of calm and release. It is the opposite of urgency."

Excerpts from Larry Dossey, M.D., *Space, Time, and Medicine.* Boulder, Colo.: Shambala Publications, 1982.

QUOTE FROM CHRISTIAN KOMOR

We are a society which values production, achievement and "getting the job done." It has become "normal" to overwork and focus on doing to the exclusion of our own being. We have, in a sense, become addicted to work and forgotten how to play for the sake of play.

Excerpt from Christian Komor, *The Power of Being: For People Who Do Too Much!* Grand Rapids, Mich.: Renegade House Productions, 1991.

and more—shape our schedules. Electric lights and global interactions have us working at all hours of the day and night. The pace at which our transactions take place are measured in nanoseconds. "Multitasking" is the norm. We e-mail our boyfriend while receiving a fax while talking on a cell phone while we have a book open that we're trying to study.

There are whole books on the subject of the frantic, crazy, stressed-out way of life that our society thinks is "normal." The point of mentioning all this is simply that you definitely should not blame yourself for feeling stressed-out in our stressed-out workaholic culture.

Oddly enough, this does not mean you are helpless to change.

The responsibility to change still lies within you.

DID YOU KNOW?

The Puritans were a particular sect, or group of sects, of Christianity. They believed that people were born inherently bad due to the "original sin" associated with Adam and Eve in the Old Testament Bible. What people should do to redeem this original sin is suffer. Suffer, suffer, suffer! The more the better! This is the attitude that shaped our work ethic because the early major industrialists were largely Puritans. Today, the orientation that says, "I'm bad and guilty and undeserving and I should work hard and toil and suffer all my life to redeem myself," is still alive and well in most of us in our society, handed down from generation to generation like bad teeth.

It just means that you say stuff like this: "Yes, all sorts of things, family things, cultural things, maybe even some genetic things brought me to where I am now (stressed-out), but the only way for me to change is to come to the position of responsibility. Being stressed-out may be 'their' fault, because I didn't know the stuff I'm learning now, but if I *stay* stressed-out, that can only be my fault."

So, you should feel totally innocent for the fact that you're stressed-out—you've grown up in a horrendously stressed-out culture and who knows what circumstances in your family. But allow me to suggest that you begin to cultivate greater and greater responsibility (i.e., empowerment) for changing your experience and for creating deep inner peace and serenity. It's the only option you've got.

HEAVY-DUTY STRESS

This is very important: There are a lot of really tough things in life that no book alone can help with. Let's call them the heavy-duty stressors. *If you are chronically depressed, or if you sometimes have suicidal thoughts, or if you are abusing—and possibly addicted to—drugs and/or alcohol, or if you have eating disorders or other compulsive behaviors, or if you're being abused (verbally, physically, sexually) you are in crisis and you need living, breathing, human help. As in therapists, counselors, that kind of thing. Really.*

These things create stress, but they usually create so much more than stress that it's almost silly to call it stress. It's like saying a Sherman tank parked on your rib cage creates stress. These things don't just create stress, they will kill you. No joking.

CHRONIC MEANNESS

Another issue that deserves its own special discussion is that of bullies, teasers, abusers and general entrapment (usually at school) with chronic meanness. For many young people this stuff is the most stressful thing in their lives, but, like addiction or abuse at home, it's really a whole different level of stress than this book is aimed at. It requires intervention.

Did you know? Many sociological surveys done over the last 30-some years show a steady increase of people reporting that they have less and less time and feel more and more frenetic, overwhelmed and out of control.

YOU'RE NOT ALONE IN FEELING STRESSED

"More than any other pollster, the Roper Organization has studied the specifics of what one Roper executive calls our 'society on the go.' This ongoing market study polls 2,000 consumers throughout the country ten times a year. Roper has been tracking the time shortage trend since their current survey began in 1973, and has noted its impact since the mid–1980s in particular. 'Our studies clearly show that people feel they have less and less time,' reported Tom Miller, editor of Ropers' Public Pulse. 'They have the impression that they have less hours and days than they used to.'

"Those polled report spending less time browsing in stores than they used to, having fewer hobbies and a declining number of 'personal interests' overall. Instead of mentioning six or seven interests they'll mention three or four.' said Miller. 'This suggests that people feel this time pressure, the increasing lack of time.'

Excerpts from Ralph Keyes, *Timelock: How Life Got So Hectic and What You Can Do about It.* New York: Ballantine Books, 1993. Courtesy, Ralph Keyes, Ballantine Books. All Rights Reserved. Reprinted with permission.

OUR FRANTICALLY PACED SOCIETY IS FAIRLY UNIQUE, IN TIME AND PLACE

"Our ancestors did not equate *hard* work with *constant* work as we so often do. . . . Their work usually consisted of bursts of intense activity followed by periods of respite. This irregular rhythm was in tune with our body's own clocks."

In describing the work of psychology professor Robert Levine, Ralph Keyes, author of *Timelock*, says, "As with Brazilians, he found that most of the nationality groups he studied (the Japanese being a notable exception) were far less time obsessed than Americans. In countries ranging from Indonesia to Italy Levine found watches less common, clocks less accurate, the pace of walking slower, and the amount of time taken to conduct a routine transaction (buying stamps at the post office) longer. He discovered that an emphasis on being punctual went hand in glove with a faster pace of life.

"Native: You Americans. You're always running around. 'Time is money.'

"Levine: But we have a finite amount of time. We don't want to squander it. If you don't use it, you lose it.

"Native: That's the whole point. You lose it by hurrying.

"The Indians produced most of what they used: pots, baskets, cloth. Presumably this took a lot of time. This is what the Johnsons assumed. It wasn't so. A typical Machiguenga adult devoted only a few hours a day to making implements, farming, or foraging. Much of their time was given over to visiting each other, or simply taking it easy.

"The Machiguenga never seemed harried. There was no word for 'worried' in their vocabulary. Nor was there one for 'time.' (They indicated periods of the day by pointing to positions of the sun.) As a result, time didn't run short for the Machiguenga. They behaved as though this commodity was abundant.

"In one setting after another he began to see a clear correlation between a relaxed pace of life and the enjoyment people seemed to be getting from their lives."

To be trapped, day after day, in contact with a person or persons who are teasing, mocking, humiliating, intimidating or otherwise abusing you—not to mention physical abuse and bullying—is horrendous and can be deeply traumatizing, creating depression, anxiety disorders and all kinds of nasty consequences. It is stress, yes, but it's so often so much larger than stress that, like I said above about *Heavy-Duty Stress,* it's almost silly to use the word. The suggestions in this book can help a little, but no young person can withstand such assaults on her personhood while her identity is developing.

What I'm getting at is that, if you're dealing with any of this "chronic meanness," you must get help. Talk to parents, talk to a trusted teacher, or school counselor. You've got to overcome the ridiculous stigma against so-called "tattling." It is *not* uncool or weak; it is what a self-respecting, intelligent, wise person does. If you must, see if you can switch schools to one where the teachers, who are being paid to maintain a safe, healthy environment for you, can do so.

Adults who sexually abuse children convince them of how bad it would be for the child to tell anybody. Wife beaters convince their wives about the same thing. This is what victimizers do to victims. You must find the courage, the support, to speak out for yourself. No one deserves the torment of chronic meanness. Sometimes people stay silent out of shame; they feel it says something bad about *them* that they're being abused! This, also, is classic "victim psychology." You must get clear that your abusers are the sick ones, the losers, the only problem. Break the silence. Talk to people. Get help. If possible, get the hell out. You are almost never as trapped and alone as you think you are, unless you yourself are enforcing that aloneness, refusing to see and consider the help and support that may be around you. Break the shame, reach out for help. These forms of abuse are no joke—most people have been through them at one time or another—and you must handle them.

A WORD ABOUT THERAPY

It's common for people who need therapy to not want to seek therapy. But professional psychological help, in our culture, is how most people get healthy, or at least how they get up onto their wobbly legs enough to begin the process. Other cultures had (or have) shamans or priests or seers or voodoo doctors or wise elders or maybe—though I grant you it's hard to imagine—families that weren't all dysfunctional.

Also, people didn't just hunker down in their own little solitary box of a house or apartment, essentially surviving on their own. There were these amazing things called communities. In these communities you'd be around not only the usual nutty uncles and friends but there'd also always be some incredibly wise, compassionate people you could go to for help. Very few of us have that anymore. Now, in this day and age and place, we've got therapists. You can love it, you can hate it, but if you're in any kind of crisis like what I mentioned above, just get one. Fast. Find a way.

If you're not in a crisis but you're just really serious about getting relaxed and unstressed and peaceful, then too, get yourself a therapist. It's a love-deprived, shame-based culture we live in and the brave ones usually put in a few years of therapy as one part of their overall intention to create deep peace and clarity in their lives.

Aren't there a lot of lame therapists out there? You betcha. There are a lot of lame everythings out there. But that's just the way it goes, and it doesn't hold much water as an excuse not to get help. There are also a lot of incredibly wise, talented and compassionate therapists out there. You just have to take the time to find them. Check out a few until you find one who fits for you. A great place to start is by asking someone you know—a friend, a friend's parent, your chiropractor, a school counselor, or teacher— to recommend a therapist. You're worth the effort. And all those dark, tangled complex thoughts and feelings that people in crisis get and that seem so horribly unique to you are what therapists deal with all day, every day.

Working sincerely and hard with real help can change everything over time; it can change your entire experience of life beyond what you can even imagine when you're smack dab in the middle of the pain.

Here's another funny thing: Your therapist doesn't even have to be a genius of insight. If you find one of these, great, but even a therapist who's just a decent, compassionate, relatively grounded person can help immensely. Oceans of stress are relieved just by speaking about it openly and freely to another caring human being; the very process of confession, of being seen and known by somebody else, someone relatively accepting and trustworthy is extremely powerful medicine. A mysterious and transformative alchemy takes place. It's very good stuff. Partake freely.

WHY BE STRESS-FREE?
(The Benefits to Being Relaxed and Carefree)

Even though it's totally okay to just want a wee little bit of stress reduction, you'll notice throughout this book that I really stand for people going for major freedom and lightness in how they feel. It is this that I am calling radiant inner peace. If I can get you looking into totally transforming your uptight life into an easy, loose, spacious life, I'll be ecstatic. Just because few people make this choice doesn't mean you shouldn't.

But why? you ask. Isn't that a whole lot of work?

Yep. It sure is. But it's infinitely easier than a life lived as a white-knuckled fist. Most people simply haven't realized this. They're too caught up hurtling down the narrow tunnel of their stressed-out lives to step back, take a breath, and really consider these things. So then, why indeed? Let's consider it.

First of all, I know full well that the way stress tears your health into shreds doesn't motivate you because deep down in your heart of hearts you are secretly certain that you're indestructible. Teenagers, as I'm sure you're aware, are famous the world over for thinking they'll never die. It's okay. I did too. So I won't try to talk you into industrial grade inner peace—radiant inner peace—to avoid health problems, back and neck pain, headaches, ulcers and other digestive problems, asthma, heart problems, fried-out adrenal glands and on and on. These will never happen to you, right? Of course not! So forget about the health benefits. Who needs 'em?

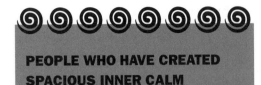

PEOPLE WHO HAVE CREATED SPACIOUS INNER CALM

▶ accomplish more.
▶ see the big picture.
▶ see the priorities in a project.
▶ have amazing relationships.
▶ are in command of themselves.
▶ are more creative.
▶ have a calm but powerful presence.

Instead, do this: Think for a moment of what you want in life. It could be good grades, it could be to master something—a sport, an art, dance, a musical pursuit, writing, whatever. It could be to snag that hot guy or girl. It could be to get along better with your family members and/or your friends. Or, though it's the very last thing any of us wants to admit (and no, it doesn't go away when you're an adult) it could be the desire to be cool, hip, popular. I know, it's annoying even to see the words in print. Becoming a deeply relaxed person makes you about a zillion times more able to create and achieve any or all of these. Without a shadow of doubt. And I don't mean maybe.

People who've created a spacious inner calm are almost superhuman. They have the concentration, the presence of mind to accomplish worlds more, in half the time, than a stressed-out person. In the short term, hour by hour, the at-ease person can stay present, effortlessly involved and focused. In the long term, over the days, weeks, and months, the relaxed person is even, solid, and steady. Stressed-out types, on the other hand, tend to have erratic bursts of marginal productivity (though they feel extremely busy) followed by exhaustion, or else their energy just strays, getting scattered in different directions.

A relaxed, quiet mind sees the big picture and very naturally sees the priorities in a project. It always easily sees what's best to do in what order and how best to do it.

As far as relationships go, relaxed people tend to have amazing relationships because they're not fretting and distracted. This means they've got the available attention for the people in their lives, which, frankly speaking, is somewhat rare. We're all used to people being too tightly wound up in their own stress to have any real energy and attention left over for us. So when somebody does, people are naturally very attracted to them. They seem like saints!

Also, when we are deeply calm, our whole being blossoms. Our face softens and relaxes, our eyes brighten and

start to twinkle and shine, we access our natural spontane-
ity and authenticity. People want to be around this sort of
presence, even if they can't say exactly why.

Another thing about a truly relaxed person is what others feel about her, instinctively—that she is in command of
herself. Her eyes are clear, awake, conscious. This person
has a calm, but powerful, commanding presence in a room.
You wanna talk about cool? Hip? Popular? Puhleaze!
Fuhgeddabowdit. James Bond? Not stressed. Even with
bullets zinging by his face and nasty scorpions scuttling
around under his shirt.

Incidentally, relaxed people also play better. They tend to
play more wholeheartedly because they're not distracted.
They're present. Since they're not uptight and tense, they're
more able to abandon themselves into whatever they're doing: play or work.

Lastly, relaxed people are generally much more creative.
A tense, agitated, distracted, contracted mind dries up the

creative storehouses. Hemingway talked of how the unconscious mind should always be working on what you're creating in its silent, mysterious depths, but when you're stressed-out, the unconscious mind is occupied with *that* instead, and the wellspring runs dry. A clear, relaxed mind opens up the floodgates to the creative juice.

You get the idea. Basically, think of anything good that you want in your life. Anything. The more deep peace and ease you create in yourself, the better you'll be able to create it. "Relaxed you" compared to "stressed-out you" is literally a genius, a Jedi knight full of energy, brilliant insight, wise perspective and uncanny intuition.

Oh yeah, and then there's that little detail of happiness, another reward of radiant inner peace. As a matter of fact, when you get right down to it, radiant inner peace—being at ease and stress-free—is just another way of saying happiness. Stress = not happy. No stress = happy.

If "happiness" doesn't seem like a very motivating reason for you to get serious about unlearning stress, it's probably just because "happiness" seems like a vague, abstract thing to you, maybe even an unrealistic one. It's such a big word it may seem a bit meaningless. And yet, everything you do, play, try to get, everything you hope for and try to do, you do ultimately because you want to be happy. Each of those things you want, later tonight, next month, next decade, you want because you believe it'll make you happy. It'll make you feel good, relieved, released, at ease, carefree. But these feelings come from within you, and not from any achievement, goal, object or attainment. The only thing standing between you and those good feelings you want is stress.

So, why be stress-free? Let's recap, shall we?

1. **To be healthy (even though you don't care)**
2. **To have healthy, fun relationships with people**
3. **To create what you want to create in life**
4. **To be hip, cool, attractive and popular**
5. **To be happy and feel good and playful and light.**

Not a shabby list, eh?

The Real Deal Solution

2

ADDRESSING THE ROOT CAUSE OF OUR STRESS

To reiterate, this second part of the book is about the root of
the whole matter of stress or rather, inner peace. It's the meat-
and-potatoes. To return to our earlier analogy, this part is
about patching the hole in the bottom of the boat to stop the
water from coming in. It's not about bailing. There are no
quick fixes in this part. None. Zero. Nada. Zippo. The quick
fixes (well, they're not all that quick) are in part three of the
book. And there's nothing wrong with quick fixes. I'm all for
'em. We all gotta bail some water out of our boat once in a
while. Or even a lot. It's just sort of silly to be doing it while
that big hole is continuously gushing more water.

So this second part of the book is where it's really at. This
is where true, deep, lasting peace, serenity, lightheartedness
and good feeling are really at. It's no small or casual matter.
Know this. This is about a whole life's work. Ongoing. Always progressing and growing, but never "perfect." It's hard
and it's slow and it's deep and it's real and it's the gold, the
best stuff of all.

Adults don't usually like to tell you this stuff because
most adults believe that teenagers will only be drawn to
what's quick and easy. This is an annoying, condescending
point of view. I don't hold it because I actually take you seri-
ously. In my opinion, one of the worst things in this country
is the "quick fix" mentality that is everywhere you look.
We've become a nation of infants, and popular culture constantly assumes—and gives us the message—that we cannot
generate the strength, the tenacity to pursue anything deeply
and truly. To persist. To persevere. To master ourselves and
the things we pursue. This message assaults us all day, every
day, on TV, on the radio, in pop music, on signs, billboards,

*. . . in this second
part, I call you
to gradually, at
your own pace,
take up the
challenge of inner
work required to
become genuinely
stress-free, deep
in your being.*

in and on busses, magazines and on and on. Quick and easy beauty, popularity, riches, toys, health, adventure, happiness (Prozac! . . . even for people who don't truly need it) and on it goes. We're supposed to run around like idiots until our dying day, manipulated by the latest slick, clever advertising assaults to buy the latest, brief hit of aliveness before getting quickly bored and moving on to the next one.

But I believe that people, maybe teenagers more than anyone, long for what is authentic, real. Not flashy and plastic, but enduring and genuine. In our heart of hearts, we yearn for depth and substance. What's more, we yearn even for the tests, trials and challenges it will take to earn them. Call me an idealist, but I'm convinced that people, especially young people, are starting to see through the whole empty, pitiful charade. And they want the real deal, even if it's tough and demanding. *Especially* if it's tough and demanding. That's why I called this second part "The Real Deal Solution."

So, in this book, especially in this second part, I call you to gradually, at your own pace, take up the challenge of inner work required to become genuinely stress-free, deep in your being. In this part of the book, I'm actually talking the real talk with you. I'm throwing down the challenge to engage the bold, heroic work that very few people, of any age, take up.

The trials, the ordeals of military training, of wilderness survival programs like Outward Bound, of times of crisis, chaos, and upheaval can test us mightily. But the journey within, to face our own "demons" and "dragons," is the ultimate adventure. To heal and transform the roots of stress requires that journey of us. Let's get down to it.

GROUND ZERO: INTENTION
The Desire to Learn a New Way Must Come From You

I need to reiterate, here, that if all you want is some symptomatic relief from your stress, just a bit less of the stuff in

your face, that's perfectly okay. We all have our own tim-
ing, our own unique process in life, and I hereby honor you
and your freedom. Anyway, ripeness is everything, as somebody famous once said. Or should've. When you've grown
ripe enough to go for radiant inner peace, great; until then,
you have my unreserved blessings in using this book only
for some very cool, snazzy, effective buckets to bail the water with.

But if you are moved toward the "deluxe package"—
the stress *prevention* package, the plug-the-hole package, really transforming the whole "stress thing" at it's gnarly little
roots; if you are ready to begin the fascinating process of
creating deep, resonant ease and peace, this radiant inner
peace I keep harping on, then the very first discussion to
have is about intention. This, dear friends, is the absolute
bottommost of all bottom lines. Intention. Aim. Desire.
That's why this chapter is the longest one in the whole
book! For good reason!

Because the whole process of creating radiant inner peace
starts with intention—yours. If you really want radiant inner
peace, want it with a burning desire, sooner or later you'll
start having it. And without that desire, no book, no technique, no system will help much. If this deep, clear intention
is awake in you, you don't "need" any *particular* method,
approach, or resource, yet you'll make use of any methods,
approaches, and resources: You'll adapt, modify, and experiment to fit your unique vision of deep inner peace.

However, most people, even those who read books on
"stress reduction," practice techniques, and who go to therapists do not have that hungry, indomitable intention. They
want the good results, but without ever finding out how
they've been creating the bad results all this time. They
want the magical cure that comes without any responsibility. Their intention is still rather casual. If you're one of
those, have no worries, mate! The answer sounds terribly
silly, but pay attention, because it's actually pretty profound. The answer is, first of all, to do this: Really, really
know that your intention is still fairly casual.

⊚ ⊚ ⊚ ⊚ ⊚ ⊚ ⊚ ⊚ ⊚ ⊚ ⊚ ⊚ ⊚

DID YOU KNOW?

The foundation principle of Psychology of Mind (known also by a number of other names including Health Realization, Philosophy of Living, and POM) is that each of us has the inborn potential for deep, buoyant mental health, and that therapy works best when it focuses on teaching health rather than just analyzing dysfunction. Hence, Psychology of Mind (POM) functions more from an educational model than a conventionally "therapeutic" model. POM teaches us about how our thinking creates our experience in life.

Dr. George Pransky, Ph.D., is one of the principal founders and originators of POM, and is the main leader in the development of POM in theory and in clinical applications. He is also an internationally respected speaker and consultant for private and government organizations. In short, George Pransky is the big cheese mucky muck of POM, who other POM practitioners sometimes secretly refer to as "King George."

Many spiritual paths and the psychology system called Psychology of Mind teach that your deepest core always naturally yearns toward health, wholeness, healing, and growth, as naturally as a plant turns toward the sun. Just as your body heals a cut or scrape, your inner self also has an inborn movement toward wellness. If you are not fully expressing this natural yearning toward vibrant wholeness, know that you must be actively *doing* something (though if you're like most of us, you're probably not conscious of it) to obstruct this innate movement toward healing and growth. In other words, you do indeed have within you that strong, muscular intention toward real freedom from stress; your so-called "laziness" is just something you're actively overlaying on top of that powerful intention. Become curious about that. Interested. "Hmmm, I wonder how I 'do' casual, lame intention. Where does that come from? What do I get out of that? How does it work?"

Maybe you'll discover attitudes deep in your noggin that say you don't "deserve" anything like radiant inner peace. Maybe you'll discover deep feelings of generalized hopelessness ("People can't really change. At least I can't.") that need to be healed. Maybe you'll discover that to accept radiant inner peace also means accepting a much larger, more capable and powerful you than you want to: too much responsibility. And you'd have to let go of the victim, self-pity role that you've gotten very used to. Who knows what you'll discover! But your attitude can move more and more toward this: "If I'm not passionately involved in creating deep serenity I must not be as motivated as I think I am. I can't quite see how I'm doing this "unmotivated-ness" yet. But I really *want* to see it. I really want to discover what that's all about for me."

They say "what you've disowned, owns you." The opposite of that is that the more conscious and aware you become of how you suppress your burning desire, the more that very consciousness and awareness allows your suppressing ways to melt, change, and move. For habitual patterns or "energy structures" to stay stuck and unmoving requires unconsciousness. Start to look, observe, notice, and become conscious. Talk about this process with others. You'll be amazed.

THE FORUM

The Forum training is an intensive weekend (and more, if you want to go on) of exploring how our beliefs, attitudes, presumptions and unconscious "life-scripts" unnecessarily limit us and our lives. The Forum was created by a man named Werner Erhardt in the early 1970s. It was originally called the EST Training, an amalgam of concepts from Eastern philosophies and Western psychotherapeutic approaches. EST was one of the central players in the early days of the "human potential movement," a pop-culture explosion of interest in personal, psychological, spiritual, and social growth which began in the late '60s and early '70s.

Once you've started to take responsibility (gently and lovingly) for your casualness in intention (and this can take a long time) the other part is, very simply, to *want* a strong, fiery intention. Long for that burning desire. Respect it. In the "Forum" training they call this "creating the space for it to be." In 12-Step programs like AA this same pattern is central: Get really clear, conscious, honest and confess where you're truly at, and then become willing for growth and change. A brilliant guy named Robert Fritz calls this "structural tension," and shows how it's the essence of the creative process. You maintain a vivid, rigorously honest awareness of your "current reality" and simultaneously, a vivid focus

12-STEP PROGRAMS

12-Step programs originated from Alcoholics Anonymous, or "AA," which was begun in the mid-1930s, by two alcoholics, Bill W. and Dr. Bob S. The philosophy they used was influenced by a spiritual movement of the era called "The Oxford Group." Essentially, AA is a fellowship of people who desire to live a sober life and they help each other to do this through many tools and approaches: the living of universal spiritual principles, regular AA meetings, and working with the 12 steps.

For most, AA is a spiritual program, only insofar as members work on trusting and surrendering to "God as we understand God" or "a power greater than ourselves"; for some, this "power greater than ourselves" is simply their AA group.

AA is the largest, most successful self-help movement in the world and no other approach to recovering from addictions has had anything even close to the success of AA. All that, and it's free! And anonymous (hence the name).

Since AA's inception, numerous other 12-Step programs based on the AA model have evolved: Narcotics Anonymous, Al-Anon (for friends, loved ones, or family members of addicts or alcoholics), Gamblers Anonymous, Spenders Anonymous, Marijuana Anonymous, Sex Addicts Anonymous, Overeaters Anonymous, Workaholics Anonymous, and Adult Children of Alcoholics.

DID YOU KNOW?

Robert Fritz is a composer, artist, writer, and entrepreneur whose work has been used by Fortune 500 companies and other organizations and groups throughout the world, and in the lives of tens of thousands of people. He is also an author whose books include *The Path of Least Resistance* and *Creating*.

on your "vision." There's a "dissonance" between those two—structural tension—that strives toward resolution: the creation of your vision.

However you describe this "equation," it is the great secret of human growth and change. First explore it and play with it and use it to cultivate a deep, serious intention about healing your stressful ways. Then use it to heal your stressful ways.

In this way, the intention to heal and the healing process itself will truly be yours. It will come from you, from your unique qualities and sensibilities. You'll be learning, experimenting, risking, and inventing things of your own.

THE GREAT, BIG, MAJOR-LEAGUE, HEAVY-DUTY SECRET

Okay, you've started to get clear and conscious about your intention now, so that it may grow strong, right?

Most excellent. Now that we've talked about that, we can jump into the very heart of the matter. And here it is: The great secret, dear friends, is that

stress comes from the inside out.

It looks the other way around, like stress comes from our evil "to-do" lists, our obligations. It looks like we're "stressed-out" because of our demented math teacher and the pure evil of SATs, or because we may have to go to the prom with a ghoulish mutant or because of our health or our grades or our poverty or our weight or our sports or our misbehaving goldfish or the wobbly leg on the kitchen table or the terrible and oppressive mystery of the scroll button on the computer. But it ain't. None of these reasons or their ugly little friends create our stress. We do. You and me. All by ourselves.

We each learned that our inner experience of stress resulted not from the circumstances of our harried lives, but from our habitual way of perceiving life. We learned that we could change our inner worlds—our feelings, our stress levels, even the speed of our lives—by tapping into a way of thinking that makes life easier, simpler, and much more enjoyable.

Excerpts from Richard Carlson and Joseph Bailey, *Slowing Down to the Speed of Life: How to Create a More Peaceful, Simpler Life From the Inside Out.* San Francisco: HarperSanFrancisco, 1997.

This is what all the great religions and spiritual systems of the world have taught for thousands of years. The biblical quote, "If thine eye offend thee, pluck it out," is not suggesting icky and messy self-mutilation; it's saying that the offensive (i.e., stressful) things you see "out there" aren't truly a problem "out there" at all—it's in how you are perceiving them. Our old friend Shakespeare tells us, through the mouth of Hamlet, that "nothing is either good nor bad (stressful or non-stressful) but thinking makes it so."

VIKTOR E. FRANKL

Viktor E. Frankl (1905–1997) was a very famous psychotherapist, one of the greatest of the 20th century. In popular culture, Frankl is best known for his landmark book, *Man's Search For Meaning* in which he (among other things) recounts his years as a prisoner in four Nazi concentration camps (including Auschwitz) and the remarkable way he maintained his dignity, integrity, spirit (and as a consequence, his health) under unimaginably horrific circumstances.

Frankl went on to develop a revolutionary approach to psychotherapy called logotherapy, whose central idea is that the *meaning* we give to our existence is what gives our life motivation, integrity, and wholeness.

Here's another thing to consider: If stress really did sort of fly in the window and come upon us, from "the world out there," then there could not be the countless people who face even the worst "stressors"—imminent death, terminal illnesses, and so on (the biggies) with utter peace and serenity. Logically, if stress comes *from* life's events, there just flat-out couldn't be such people. But there are. You can read all about them in all sorts of places like Bernie Siegel, M.D.'s books, or Richard Moss's, to start with.

If stress happened to us, there couldn't be guys like Viktor Frankl, a prisoner in a Nazi concentration camp during World War II who handled the inconceivable horrors of life with nearly miraculous equanimity and presence. If things like torture, death, and catastrophic illness can be faced with profound inner calm and peace, then so can things like grades, romance, and other ordinary daily life stressors. Well, okay, maybe not romance.

But this is real stuff. There really are lots of people who face unimaginable trials, truly heavy stuff, with inner tranquility and ease and grace, and there are people who have a conniption fit because they get put on hold on the phone. If you really look at these things you start to get it that either stress or peace comes from inside us, not at all from things and events "out there."

Of course you can see it in "the little things" too. One person can be late for a vital appointment and stuck in a traffic jam and totally freak out. Another, in the same situation, can shrug and thoroughly relax and enjoy the ride.

The first person says to himself, while his head explodes, "If I'm late for this interview at this college, they'll never accept me, and if I don't get into this college, I won't have the great career, and if I don't have the great career, I'll have a ruined life," etcetera.

The second person doesn't think anything, really, because she's just in the present moment and she knows she has no idea what will unfold in the future; it's all sheer imagination. That's just plain old true. So why think about what's totally, completely unknowable? But even if she *did* think about it, her thinking might go something like this: "I'll get there at the exact same time whether I'm frantic and stressed-out or whether I'm calm and happy, so why not enjoy myself and have fun during this ride instead? It's outside my control, so why would I possibly get uptight? What will be will be. Plus, by relaxing and enjoying myself, I'll be thinking much more clearly, loosely, and creatively, and have great composure when I get there, so if there is any way to save the interview, I'll have a much better chance of doing so and I'll make a much better overall impression. And, even if the interview truly is blown, life is a totally creative, unpredictable, and mysterious affair and who knows where my path will twist and turn? It'll come out *some* way, and out of the ashes new things and possibilities rise up, and how fascinating that will be! And last of all, my wholeness and happiness always lies in me, and only in me, right now, in the present moment. My wholeness and happiness never lies outside of me, in what college or career I'm in, so while I'd prefer this college, I certainly don't *need* it to turn out in any particular way to give me my okayness and contentment. That's inherent."

There really are people like this, who live like this! And no, you absolutely do *not* have to be born that way or brought up that way.

QUOTAGE FROM RICHARD CARLSON AND JOSEPH BAILEY, TWO POM (PSYCHOLOGY OF MIND) GUYS:

"Lifestyle changes alone rarely make a real difference. You can rearrange the externals of your life in a radically different way, but you always take your thinking with you. If you are a hurried, rushed person in the city, you'll also be a hurried, rushed person in the country.

"If we believe that our feelings are determined by outside forces, it follows that we will seek something equally external in response. As we gain an understanding of our psychological experience, however, we can recognize that the actual *source* of our experience is always our thinking. Thus we can begin to restore the power in our lives."

Excerpts from Richard Carlson and Joseph Bailey, *Slowing Down to the Speed of Life: How to Create a More Peaceful, Simpler Life From the Inside Out.* San Francisco, CA: HarperSanFrancisco, 1997. Courtesy, Richard Carlson and Joseph Bailey, HarperCollins Publishers. All Rights Reserved. Reprinted with permission.

Being stressed-out is not *"just the way you are."*

Yes, some people are luckier than others in this way and due to genes or upbringing they *do* find it naturally easier to be peaceful, calm, and relaxed. How nice for them. And who cares? That has nothing to do with anything.

Where would I possibly find enough leather
With which to cover the surface of the earth?
But (wearing) leather just on the soles of my shoes
Is equivalent to covering the earth with it.

Likewise it is not possible for me
To restrain the external course of things;
But should I restrain this mind of mine
What would be the need to restrain all else?

Excerpt from Acharya Shantideva,
A Guide to the Bodhisattva's Way of Life.
Dharamsala: Library of Tibetan Works & Archives, 1979.

The only fact that you and I need concern ourselves with is this: Countless people have changed, are changing, and will change from stressed-out types to relaxed, at-ease types. We do not only grow and change in childhood and then stop, no matter how many stuffy, stodgy, old Freudians or behaviorists say we do. The stream of human growth and evolution is constant, and we are always standing in a brand new moment with countless unimagined possibilities. This change is real, concrete, utterly doable, and eminently possible. Difficult? Yep. Pretty rare? You betcha; not many people are willing to work for their serenity and well-being. But those few who do receive the fruits. You can, too.

IT'S NOT THE STUFF I HAVE TO DO THAT'S STRESSING ME OUT; IT'S WHO I THINK I AM!

As you start to discover that stress comes from the inside out, you'll also discover that there are different layers of how it comes from the inside out. Just about the deepest level of how we create our own stress is the level of personal identity; who we think we are.

Take perfectionism for example. Perfectionism, like the name implies, is the feeling that whatever we do we have to do it perfectly, or pretty darn close. It is an incredibly stressful way to go through life. For example, perfectionists are anxious before a date because they feel tremendous pressure to be amazing and wonderful; they're anxious before a test at school or before an athletic competition or a musical or a theatrical performance for the same reason. They're uptight and tense about the paper they have to write, the assignment they have to do. They may even be stressed about a party because they put such pressure on themselves to be cool, charming, and charismatic. Perfectionism comes from the belief that we're somehow not good enough; that we're not totally okay and whole and loveable exactly as we are, full of human imperfection. The belief that, to be okay, to be enough, we must be perfect.

Deep down, it's a belief that while others can be imperfect and still be loveable, we cannot.

Another way of talking about perfectionism is to talk about self-imagery. Here's what happens: Most of us are taught by our parents that we're not good enough; we're not okay and worthy and loveable, fully and totally just as we are. They make this mistake in total innocence, because their parents did the same to them, and their parents' parents did the same to them, and so on, way on back. (How all this started is the subject of zillions of books and theories and arguments of every shape and kind—we don't have time to go there now.) All our parents, in fact all parents period, did the best they could with what they had. It is spectacularly non-helpful to "blame" our parents, or anyone at all.

To heal from our compulsive doing and find that sense of self-ownership and fulfillment, we need to let go of our shame. Shaming ourselves further about the situation and viewing ourself as defective only gets us more "stuck." Compulsive doing is a process based on shame and low self-esteem—and it thrives on it. The power of being arises through acceptance of who we are and who we are not.

Excerpt from Christian Komor,
The Power of Being: For People Who Do Too Much!
Grand Rapids, Mich.: Renegade House Productions, 1991.

But the fact of the matter is that most of us ended up feeling unworthy deep down inside. If our family had some alcoholism or other heavy-duty dysfunction, we probably even have shame in us.

Shame is the feeling that there is something really wrong with us; it's the feeling, or thought, that we are somehow damaged, uniquely flawed. Many, many people suffer from shame. Maybe most.

When people grow up believing the yucky lie that they're somehow not okay and loveable, they sometimes just go through their lives feeling inferior and flawed. Other people react to their shame differently; they start to form what psychoanalyst Karen Horney (very famous big shot) calls an "idealized image" of themselves, to compensate for how unworthy they *really* feel. Deep, deep down they never really buy that they are this idealized image for a minute, but they fool themselves pretty good. A great barometer to know if you have an idealized image of yourself is if you often think you're better than other people. Or "secretly" better.

Beneath the idealized image, and driving it, is the "despised image." This image is the one we secretly, mostly unconsciously feel that we are. It is as false as the idealized image. Neither one is us. They're both fantasies. But—and here's the point—living with these images is extremely stressful. Awful. Exhausting. It's a terrible torment of constant stress, but it's a torment many of us don't even know we're stuck in! We just think this is "normal"! We automatically presume that this is how everyone experiences himself or herself. (We'll get more into this in the next chapter.)

But for now just know that it's a tremendous energy drain to walk around feeling shame and/or maintaining shame's mask, the idealized image, always scared of it being seen through, and always running from that "despised image."

It's like going through your life carrying an obese, smelly, sweaty witch on your back 24 hours a day.

We can all live without that.

Your truest self, your untouchable, inherent health would smile and say, before a big test at school, "I studied as much as I realistically could, given everything else going on in my life and given my own limitation as a fallible human being, and I'll do however good I do. Period. And that's that. And I'll just simply take whatever consequences come with that. What's to be stressed about? Whatever the results, my fundamental okayness and loveableness and wholeness is never, ever at stake. Never."

If you are perfectionistic—as really almost everyone is—and maybe have some shame and some idealized images of yourself and despised images and all of that, you must understand that you can heal and grow and change. As you read that, you may hear a nasty little voice, or maybe it's just a feeling, that communicates, "Maybe it's possible for other people to heal and grow and change, but it's not possible for me." That's just shame. That's exactly what shame says. That's all it knows how to say. And it's exactly, precisely what everyone's shame says. That's the amazing thing about it. It is laughably predictable.

Understanding that stress, for the most part, begins with our thoughts and beliefs is the first step in figuring out ways to manage it effectively.

One of the biggest stumbling blocks to letting our spirituality flourish and to experiencing inner peace comes from ignoring one of the most critical relationships we have--our relationship with ourselves. So much of our pain and suffering comes from feeling unworthy and undeserving of love.

Excerpt from Lori Leyden-Rubenstein,
The Stress Management Handbook.
New Canaan, Conn.: Keats Publishing, 1998.

Of course it does take work, application, tenacity. It is not easy. You must, little by little, at your own pace, uncover your own inner warrior to bravely tame and befriend the dragon of shame and inadequacy beliefs. Remember our chapter on intention? Now may be an excellent time to skim over it again.

In this book, I'm trying not to take up sides too much with specific approaches or systems of healing ourselves, because different ones work better for different people. If you gradually fuel your intention to heal your shame, if you stoke the flames of your desire and take little baby steps, you'll very naturally start to investigate which approaches are right for you.

When it comes to shame, a little book like this cannot, in itself, do much, but it can point the way toward many wonderful resources and approaches that can do plenty. In general, working through shame requires a good, trusted therapist. (See *A Word about Therapy,* page 11.)

At the very least, heartfelt opening to, and bonding with, supportive, loving people is crucial, as well as unburdening the soul by talking about your most secret hurts and fears. In AA they say, "We're only as sick as the secrets we keep." Confession to accepting, trustworthy people is amazingly powerful. Twelve-Step groups can be extraordinarily effective in dealing with shame. If you cannot afford a therapist, or are simply unready for that, I would definitely suggest finding a 12-Step group.

If your stress and shame manifests in any overt addictive process, there's probably a meeting for it. There's Overeaters Anonymous, Workaholics Anonymous, Gamblers Anonymous, Spenders Anonymous, Sex Addicts Anonymous (which includes pornography, like, say, Internet porn) and of course, Alcoholics Anonymous and Narcotics Anonymous. If you don't have an overt addictive process, check out an ACA meeting (Adult Children of Alcoholics) or an Al-Anon meeting. Al-Anon is for people who have a loved one, friend or family, who's an alcoholic or drug addict. Do a Web search, or some areas have an Alcoholics Anonymous Intergroup in the phone book that can help direct you. That last word that all these meetings have in common—anonymous—means that nobody ever tells anyone in any way, shape, or form anything about who goes to their meeting or what was talked about. It stays totally, 100% confidential.

If you are willing to make this brave, hero's journey to begin to heal your shame (and the extremely brutal perfectionism it causes) an excellent book to begin with is *Healing the Shame That Binds You* by John Bradshaw.

KNOW YOUR NORMAL

There's a wise man named George Pransky who teaches frequently about finding out what your normal is. He's talking about the fact that most of us are *always* under a lot of stress but we don't even know it. We only notice it when it's at its very worst; when it builds to a fevered pitch. But, you see, the rest of the time we're stressed-out, too, but we don't even know it because it's all we've ever known.

Consequently, we're so used to it that it's "normal" to us! So maybe we're walking around sort of fretting about whether the group we like to hang out with really accepts us and includes us, but we don't even know that we're walking around fretting. Even though it's actually a very unhappy activity! We're not even aware that we're really uptight all the time, with a busy, racing mind, because we have nothing to compare it to;

we just assume that everyone feels this way; that this is just "how life feels."

We assume it so deeply that it never even occurs to us to ask the question. As Pransky says, we are like a fish in water.

But, he says, it is crucial that we "discover our normal," that we begin to discover the state of anxiety we've been walking around in without even knowing it, and *not* just in our really low, most "stressed-out" times, but essentially *all the time*. As we do this, we start to gain some distance from it. It doesn't have the same hold upon us at all. And it starts to change.

Unbeknownst to people living in chronic stress, this stress is generated by low level thought processes like worry and bother. The people living in chronic stress do not recognize the existence of these processes because they attribute the resultant stress and tension to the inherently stressful nature of their pursuits. Living with stress is like being an active, strong person who, without awareness, wears a weighted backpack, thinking that accompanying stress and strain is the force of gravity.

Excerpt from George S. Pransky,
***The Renaissance of Psychology.* New York:**
Sulzburger & Graham Publishing, 1998.

In Psychology of Mind, the system Dr. Pransky teaches, and in numerous other religious, spiritual, and philosophical systems, they make it abundantly clear that within you and all people is a boundless wellspring of inner mental health, good feeling, deep wholeness, profound wisdom, creativity, clarity, and compassion. No matter how buried it gets through life traumas and unfun mental habits, it's always there within us, because it is our deepest and truest nature. The rest is garbage, delusion, and bold-faced lies.

The idea here is that this endless wellspring is our natural state, and so we don't really have to do things to "create it" or make it come into being. We don't have to generate it or build it or even grow it. Rather, we have to *stop* doing things mentally, with our thinking. We have to find out what we do from hour to hour to obstruct this wellspring, to cover it up. In Tibetan Buddhism, they use the image of the sun, teaching that our radiant inner well-being is like the sun. No matter how many "clouds" of painful thinking or habits we put in front of the sun, it's always shining.

The more we learn to take that step backward and see "our normal" the more we go, "*Wow*! Look at how uptight I'm always making myself by how I think . . . and I had no idea! Damn!" And the more we see how we alone are always creating that uptightness by our thinking (we'll get to that later), the more our natural inner wellspring of peace, wisdom, and humor spontaneously comes to the front. We don't have to "make" it come to the front. Awareness of what we're up to is the key. The more deeply we see the stressful "normal" we're always creating for ourselves, the more relief we get. And it's a funny thing, but you can't "force" this seeing. Like, if you're stressed-out and you want that feeling to go away, you can't just say to yourself, "well, this is all just coming from my own thinking." No matter how many times you say this to yourself, it just isn't the same as *actually* seeing it. *Actually seeing it* is a little shift that happens when you want it and respect it enough.

MORE FROM DR. GEORGE PRANSKY:

"No matter how poor quality a person's thinking might be at a given time, if the person recognizes that it is just thought and that the experience is linked to that thought, the person will ultimately not feel threatened, frightened or at risk because he is having that momentary experience."

Excerpt from George S. Pransky, *The Renaissance of Psychology*. New York: Sulzburger & Graham Publishing, 1998.

Dr. Pransky teaches that there really is no single "method" or "technique," funny as it sounds. You just have to want it. Just like we talked about fierce intentions. Know that you have a "normal" that you haven't seen yet, and that it is creating the way everything looks for you. Then desire to see it. Intend to see it. Value and respect the recognizing of this "normal." Reflect lightly, with a loose, relaxed, gentle touch on these ideas, trusting that your psyche has immense, unfathomable healing wisdom just like your body does. It'll happen for you. It'll happen more if you really drench your brain in these truths. Spend time reading a Psychology of Mind book. It'll help push the process along.

It'll happen in layers and it gets better and better little by little, over time. Each time you get a shift in your awareness and see the nasty tenseness that you used to think was "normal" you'll be tempted to think, "Okay, now I'm done. Now I'm just feeling how life really, plain old actually feels." Then a month or a year later, *zowee*, a sudden, forehead slapping insight will rock your world and you won't be able to *believe* that you thought that anxious, stressful state of mind was "normal," the way "life just feels!" You will laugh sheepishly at yourself, even while you're starting to do it again, starting to think, "Okay, but now *this time*, I've settled into the *real* reality; it's not me and my thinking making life feel how it feels, rather, this *is* how life feels." And so on. All of this means that there's no end to the depths of peace, serenity, and freedom we can feel. It is endless. It's a very big deal. Perhaps the biggest. It is a worthy exploration.

THE BUSY MIND AND THE QUIET MIND

For the person who wants to get rid of stress and create peace and serenity, one way to think about your "normal"

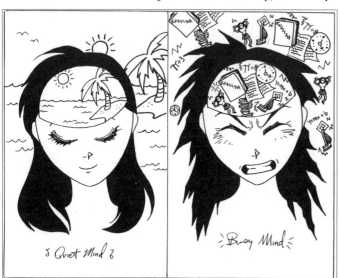

is from the angle of "busy mind" versus "quiet mind." Dr. Pransky describes how the busier and noisier your mind is, the busier and more chaotic your life appears to be; even time is experienced totally differently—to the busy mind, time seems to race by. He frequently points to early childhood when a day seemed to last forever because your mind was relaxed and free and clear. Psychology of Mind is very big on this point:

No matter how frantic and frenetic your life appears to be, it's really an illusion—it's your busy, racing, cluttered thinking creating the uncanny appearance that it's busy, racing, and cluttered "out there" in our world.

It's like you have goggles over your eyes that make the world appear frantic, but you don't even know you have them on. Those goggles are your "normal."

Tremendous relief and freedom starts to blossom when you start to catch onto this little bit of wisdom. It's an amazingly big deal. And it happens in layers: first you get small insights where you get a little bit of space between you and your busy mind "stress goggles," where you see that, all along, your stress has been coming from your own thinking that you didn't even know you were doing. Then you see it even more clearly. And the more you take that backward step to see your busy mind, the more your quiet mind will naturally blossom. Because the quiet mind is our natural state. The busy mind is unnatural—we have to "learn it." And it is exhausting, scary, distracted, incredibly ineffective in the world, and extremely unhealthy. The emotions that come with the busy mind are ones like anxiety, fear, frustration, anger, and depression.

The quiet mind is the mind of deep, spontaneous wisdom, boundless creativity, fresh new ideas and perspectives, clarity and effortless, effectiveness in our day. With a quiet mind, life seems to happen at a slow, graceful, easy, spacious pace. The emotions that come with the quiet mind are gratitude, enthusiasm, love, humor, humility, and serenity.

The fear or anger that comes from trying to live up to our "idealized image" (or, we could say, from trying to run from our "despised self" image) can kick us into the racing, busy mind. Sometimes you can find your way back to a more quiet, spacious mind just by really seeing—I mean *really* seeing—that your mind is busy and racing. But at other times maybe you'll need to really feel into the

AND HERE'S SOME MORE MOST EXCELLENT WISDOM FROM GEORGE S. PRANSKY, BIG-LEAGUE POM GUY

"In 1976, a colleague, Dr. Roger Mills, and I had the occasion to observe, over several months, people who lived in mental health brackets free from chronic stress. . . . Our observations of these people led us to the following conclusions:

1. They attended to their mind the way people attend to their bodies to avoid injury. They saw stress as a warning signal that they were abusing their mental health, just as people would see physical pain as a signal that they were abusing their bodies.

2. They did not exhibit a stress factor, even as they lived fully involved and productive lives. They lived with a sense of ease; for them, feelings of anxiety, tension and pressure were the exception rather than the norm.

3. They avoided *processing* thinking, like worry and bother that would lower their level of well-being. In fact, they used negative and positive feelings as a compass to guide them towards *free-flowing* thinking and optimum psychological functioning.

4. They were aware of the problems caused by overactive minds. They had discovered that overactive minds create unnecessary stress, lower the quality of thought processes, and create that scattered, hectic inner state that puts us under unnecessary pressure. They did their best to keep their thinking at a sane pace and resisted the temptation of having too much on their minds at once.

5. The avoidance of overactive thinking and the avoidance of thought processes that lower their level of well-being gave them what we would later refer to as good mental hygiene. They minimized the amount of extraneous thought and therefore maximized their capacity to have their minds free and clear to enjoy the moment.

continued . . .

emotional reality of your idealized image and the pain beneath it. Then, especially if you can speak vulnerably and deeply to another about it, from your heart, there will usually be a feeling of relief, of softening and a settling down and quieting of the mind. Since the quiet mind is your most natural state, and like a cork in water, is always trying to bob back up, you can access it in many ways. If you decide you want to, very badly, you will create and find and invent your own ways.

6. They had an intriguing combination of calmness and vitality. They had an intense involvement in life, yet they had a sense of calm and ease.

7. Their "normal" use of the mind was different from the use with which we were accustomed. Our thinking was more intense and analytical (what we would later recognize as predominantly *processing* thinking), while theirs was more relaxed and open-ended (what we would later recognize as predominantly *free-flowing* thinking). They had a way of seeing to the heart of the matter, seeing the big picture.

8. Their relationships reflected this higher order thinking. They tended to be compassionate of other people's frailties, rather than being resentful. They were graceful in navigating individual differences and differences of opinions.

9. They lived in feelings of well-being that were not easily lost, even in the face of adversity."

"Although Jason had an intense habit of worry for years he was totally unaware that such a habit existed in him. He had grown accustomed to it. He had developed a coping mechanism—obsessing about his life—that gave him temporary relief from his painful feelings.

"To feel anxious and fearful was 'normal' for Jason. It looked to him that he had a realistic view of what appeared to him to be a frightening world. His habit was to selectively see what might go wrong and then do what he could to prevent it. He noticed and remembered problems that others had so that he could prevent those in his own life. When things went well for him he merely breathed a sigh of relief. When things went badly he dwelled on those events long after the event was over. With his perceptions and memories so focused on problems and negative outcomes, it is no wonder that Jason saw the world as a fearful place. His obsession with caution and concern seemed appropriate under the circumstances."

Excerpt from George S. Pransky, *The Renaissance of Psychology.* New York: Sulzburger & Graham Publishing, 1998.

NON-ATTACHMENT (INVESTMENT VS INVOLVEMENT)

In the elite levels of sport psychology, the stuff world-class athletes work with, what they've found out is that when you are over-attached to winning, when you invest your happiness or your self-worth in "winning" you actually play worse. And of course, as a fringe benefit, you're uptight and miserable while you do it. This is something known and taught in Eastern philosophies (including in the martial arts and so on) for thousands of years. The Psychology of Mind people talk about investment vs. involvement. The way George Pransky puts it, the secret of being effective in life is to have very *low* investment (attachment) but very *high* involvement. This is also the secret to being relaxed, at ease, peaceful, and calm. Big test? Big date?

> ... the secret of being effective in life is to have very *low* investment (attachment) but very *high* involvement.

Tons of obligations and work? The idea here is to cultivate the feeling that your okayness and loveableness and worth is totally untouchable by *any* outcome, good or bad. Bad won't hurt it. Good won't help it. Your happiness and wholeness is inherent in you, innate, inborn, exactly as you are right now. And no "doing" can ever increase or decrease it. It has nothing, and I mean nothing, to do with what you do. Those people who learn this attitude have happy, successful, vibrant lives, and those who don't, don't.

Nobody else can grant this to you or "give you permission" for it. It can't be "earned." Egotistic swagger, arrogance or cockiness is as much the opposite of this deep knowing of wholeness (remember the idealized image?) as is open self-denigration.

Curiously enough, this non-attachment does not leave people complacent and unmotivated. Paradoxically, complacency comes from *over*investment! Because when you're overinvested in something, you say to yourself (unconsciously, of course) "this would be too painful/embarrassing/disappointing to try and then fail at, so it's much safer to just not try at all."

But when you're *truly* not attached to the outcome (as opposed to just putting on an "I don't care" attitude) but really emotionally not attached one way or the other, your natural state is to be wholeheartedly involved in whatever is in front of you. Once again, look at young children. Look at how wholehearted they are about everything they do. And, while you're at it, look at what an amazing learning curve they have. Little kids learn new skills about a zillion times faster than the rest of us (take language as an example). The less attached we are to outcomes (you can't control the outcomes, only your own effort) the more relaxed, open, at ease, you are. So not only are you happier but you have natural perspective, more creativity, intuition, a wider view.

How? Well, there are just four quick and easy steps. Just kidding!!! C'mon, you didn't really expect me to say something like that, did you? This "non-attachment" is not easy stuff. It's a sign of great self-mastery. A life's work. Non-attachment (or involvement without investment) is the natural expression of a person who has learned that their worth, value, wholeness and happiness comes from deep within, from their own pure, simple, inherent beingness.

If you've got the perfectionism bad, you'll even use stuff like being overinvested/attached to beat yourself up about. "Look at how much I'm failing at not caring about failing! Damn me!" This is painful, silly, and unproductive.

To move toward non-attachment, as in all other things, intend it with all your heart; be infinitely, wildly, unreasonably patient, loving, and gentle toward yourself at all times; recruit help. Know that like any other part of mental health, non-attachment is not an end point, it's just a direction, an orientation.

That said, you could feed the fire of your longing with books and listening to tapes about non-attachment, and

NON-ATTACHMENT AND MARTIAL ARTS

For thousands of years, masters of the martial arts have taught that non-attachment is the supreme secret of effectiveness in combat. In modern days, people who study martial art for more recreational purposes may strive toward non-attachment to winning or losing. And professional sport psychologists get paid big bucks to teach pro athletes this same wisdom about non-attachment being the secret to effective performance. In ancient days, with warriors such as the Samurai, the goal was non-attachment not only to winning or losing, but also to living or dying! The master warriors and martial artists knew that this non-attachment resulted in deep inner balance, almost super-human clarity and a profound ability to stay perfectly focused in the present moment. Being attached—to winning or even to surviving—creates an anxiety, a tension about "the outcome," which is in the future; this is a distraction from the dynamic, immediate, living, present moment of combat. It seems incredibly odd, but the less attached you are to a particular outcome, the more your energy, focus and attention is freed up, right now, to be creating what you've chosen to create. This kind of non-attachment takes great self-mastery, great mental training, but it truly is available to all of us, to anyone who truly wants it.

Do not confuse "non-attachment" with "not caring." They are opposite of each other. The non-attached person does whatever they're doing with total focus, total energy, total immersion in each present moment (which, by the way, is all there ever is)—it's being attached to the outcome that distracts us out of the present moment.

WISE THOUGHTS

- The wise person is focused on the art of living.

- The wise person is passionate about learning and flowing with the deep principles by which life unfolds.

- The wise person is about a more vivid expansion of the present moment and does not fixate on thoughts of better future moments.

- The wise person is invested in the process of self-understanding, growth, and self-mastery.

- The wise person knows that fame and fortune don't create happiness.

- The wise person knows that happiness is a matter of the heart.

- The wise person knows that life is an endless adventure of unfolding who and what you are.

people who've achieved profound levels of it. For example, the *Tao Te Ching* is an ancient, classic Chinese text by Lao-tzu (sometimes spelled tsu or tse) full of beautiful, semi-poetic, metaphoric stanzas that'll give you some serious food for thought. It's amazing.

SPIRITUALITY

This business of non-attachment raises the question: if I'm not invested in or attached to the outcome of the circumstances of my everyday life (grades, careers, relationships, etc.) then what *am* I invested in?

Throughout history, the wise have invested themselves in being rather than doing, even though they outwardly may "do" as much as—or more—than anyone else. Their interest is in the process of living and growing, the art of living, rather than any of the particular, ever-changing ingredients on the stage. Their passion is about learning and flowing with the deep principles by which life unfolds. They're interested in surrendering to the deep currents of life even while working creatively within them, with whatever life gives them.

They're always all about a vaster, more vivid expansion of the present moment, rather than fixating upon thoughts of better future moments. They're invested in the process of self-understanding, growth, learning, and self-mastery.

They have their preferences for particular circumstances and maybe they work dynamically to bring them about, with all the same projects and involvements as everyone else. These folks create full careers and rich relationships and pursue arts, hobbies, travel, education and so on, and they enjoy them thoroughly, but all the while what they're *really* up to is something inside themselves, the high art of relaxing more and more into the flow of life; cultivating the inner experience of trust, love, consciousness, and spontaneous joy for no reason.

They know that life is a heart matter, not a "get stuff" matter, and that no circumstances, no matter how idyllic, give happiness. Rather, you must start from happiness and then create your life. Being rich, famous and successful won't make you happy. Check out some biographies of rich, famous, successful people, people who achieved all the things you think will make you happy once *you* achieve them. You will notice that most of them are horrendously miserable; many were so miserable they got super-ugly drug or booze addictions and died because of them, or even committed suicide. Of course, all of this is common knowledge, but most people just assume, for some mysterious reason, that *they* would be different. Almost nobody really stops and thinks hard and long about it, really reflects on it and gets the message: no goal, no achievement, no attainment, no success will ever, ever "make you happy." Absolutely, positively, unequivocally no way. Never ever.

Instead, cultivate this attitude: Yes, of course have goals, dreams, projects, involvements, but your main concern, your main passion and interest is the endless adventure of unfolding who and what you are. Even though you may also be a painter, a photographer, a dancer or a musician, your real art is the art of emotionally surrendering to life. So what if the world around you gets busier and busier with frantic, meaningless "doing." You're more interested in cultivating your beingness.

The word, "beingness" is not in the dictionary, but it's all over the place in popular human potential books. It refers to the soft, spacious feeling of being simply present, aware, awake, gently attentive to the unfolding moment, happy and whole just to be alive.

Many people refer to all this stuff I've been describing as "spirituality." Spirituality is about cultivating your spirit; that quality of buoyancy, lightness, compassion, and happiness that is our truest essence. Spirituality is about living from the heart, from the feeling of the Mystery of everything and anything. It's about the free and quiet mind. It's about that natural feeling that bubbles up and makes you want to serve people, happily and simply. Spirituality is about the great and fascinating process of opening more and more fully into Life.

People who are all about spirituality may look like they're doing what everyone else is doing, but they're actually playing a totally different game. This buffers them from life's inevitable ups and down, stresses and strains. It's almost like a mutant superpower from a comic book hero. Because their happiness comes from an inexhaustible, invisible wellspring inside themselves that no events, no disasters, no failures can touch. It's the spirit.

Whatever happens, if they fail a class, if they don't get into any of the colleges they want to, if their girlfriend dumps them, if their parents seem to be acting like

We have forgotten that our only goal is to live and that we live each day and that at every hour of the day we are reaching our true goal if we are living. . . . The days are fruits and our role is to eat them.

—Jean Giono

Excerpt from Stephan Rechtschaffen, M.D., *Timeshifting: Creating More Time to Enjoy Your Life.* New York: Doubleday, 1996.

nutballs, these are all just "grist for the mill," just more lessons in surrendering and letting go; more lessons in how to stop making pain out of the present moment by imaginary thoughts about the future; more opportunities for self-understanding, self-mastery, and growth.

SURRENDER

Central to most paths of spirituality is this business I've mentioned several times about surrender. It's a very misunderstood word. It does not mean quitting or giving up. You can work with fierce energy to achieve something while your head is contracted into a tight ball of concern and stress. Or you can work with fierce energy to achieve something while your inner attitude says, with a trusting, merry shrug, "Thy will be done." Surrender has nothing to do with action and behavior. It's an inner attitude of letting go of your worry, concern, and attachment while you go about your life. It's letting go of the inner struggles. It's about your thinking and paradoxically it releases tremendous energy for working toward your goals.

In the 12-step approaches (originated by AA) for example, the third step goes: "Made a decision to turn our will and our lives over to the care of God as we understood God." And, the Serenity Prayer, which you've probably seen and heard many times, sums it up quite nicely: "God, grant me the serenity to accept the things I cannot change, the courage to change the things I can, and the wisdom to know the difference."

If you have trouble with the "G" word, or even the whole "G" idea, you can still receive the extraordinary peace and freedom of surrender. Duh! Surrender is about a feeling available to all of us: it doesn't care what you call it.

If you really want to, you can gradually start to discover all sorts of surprising things about your own thinking that you had just never seen before. For example,

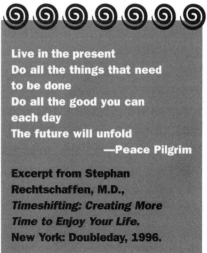

Live in the present
Do all the things that need to be done
Do all the good you can each day
The future will unfold
                    —Peace Pilgrim

Excerpt from Stephan Rechtschaffen, M.D., *Timeshifting: Creating More Time to Enjoy Your Life.* New York: Doubleday, 1996.

ZEN BUDDHISM

In the vast majority of Buddhist sects, and certainly those that are popular in the United States, the Buddha is not thought of as anything like a deity or a god. The Buddha was simply a man who "woke up," a Spiritually Awakened or Enlightened man. This Awakened State is as dramatically different from our ordinary state as the ordinary waking state is from the sleeping state. The result is indescribable freedom, peace, joy and compassion for all beings. This Spiritually Awakened State is what Buddhism is all about.

There are many different sects of Buddhists. Zen and Tibetan Buddhism are currently enjoying a virtual explosion of popularity in the West. They are both incredibly rich, diverse, elegant systems. Both emphasize, among many other things, living fully and wholeheartedly in the present moment. This "being in the present moment" is one important dimension of both Zen and Tibetan Buddhist meditation practices.

in the "Know Your Normal" and "Quiet Mind" sections, we talked about finding out just how busy and crazy and noisy our minds always are, but we just thought it was normal all this time. Well, another thing we can discover—I first read about this from a Spiritual Master named Adi Da Samraj—is that almost all our thoughts are about trying to control things in our lives. This is a key insight. What you don't usually notice is that thinking about the things in your life cannot and does not control them in any way, shape or form. As a matter of fact, another way of describing "letting go" or "surrender" is to stop thinking about it. But not like when a great movie distracts us for a couple hours. I'm talking about an emotional willingness to let go so that your whole body releases and your mind becomes more quiet and soft.

And don't tell me how "useful" and "productive" that endless, repetitive mulling is. 'Cuz it ain't! You know how long it actually takes to assess a situation and decide a course of action? About five or ten minutes at most. You either have the necessary information to decide a course of action or you don't. If you do, decide and it's done. No more mulling. If you don't, then again, you just don't, and it's done. No more mulling. You either do an action right now or you LET IT GO, and allow the mind to be quiet, open, receptive, responsive, and wise.

I don't mean to make it sound easy. It's absolutely not, and that's my point. It's just that the *very* first thing you *must* do is get rid of the belief that all that tense mulling going on in your skull 24/7 is useful or necessary or helpful. You have to lose all respect for the stressful, circular thought loops in your head.

You will have no peace as long as some tiny shadowy part of you goes, "Yeah, but if I *don't* think about this stuff, won't I get less done? Won't I lose track of important threads in my life? Won't my life spin wildly out of control?"

In POM, they talk about coming to a point of respect for the quiet, released mind; wanting it, yearning for it from deep within. In 12-Step systems, they use different language to describe the same thing. They talk about becoming *willing* to "let go and let God." If you are un-willing to let go of your stressful thoughts, the change will never come.

THE PRESENT MOMENT

Still another way to talk about essentially the same thing as surrender and letting go is staying in the present moment. Zen Buddhists (and other Buddhist types, too) are big on this angle. They noticed that the chronic, mulling thinking we're always doing tends to be about two things, neither of which exist: the past and the future. They point out that all there ever actually is, all that is real, is the now. This. Present. Moment. The time when you read the sentence two sentences back is now completely gone. It exists only as a memory. A thought. There is only this moment and now this moment and now this moment.

> The miracle is not to walk on water. The miracle is to walk on the green earth in the present moment, to appreciate peace and beauty that are available now. . . . We need only to find ways to bring our body and mind back to the present moment so we can touch what is refreshing, healing and wondrous.
>
> —**Thich Nhat Hanh**
>
> Excerpt from Stephan Rechtschaffen, M.D., *Timeshifting: Creating More Time to Enjoy Your Life.* New York: Doubleday, 1996.

Just reading or talking or thinking about it doesn't cut through very much. Liking the idea of "staying in the present moment," agreeing with it intellectually, doesn't feel any different. But when you allow this business of "staying in the present moment" to become a burning passion, things start to change in your deepest experience and feeling of life. The people who do get intensely involved in this art of living in the present almost always end up practicing meditation, but we'll talk about that later. The present moment opens up, becomes vast and slow and full, rich with textures, resonances, and feeling-tones. Stress is totally gone. You're absorbed in whatever you're doing. Relaxation pours through you. Life touches you

DID YOU KNOW?

Thich Nhat Hanh is a poet and Zen master, and was chairman of the Vietnamese Buddhist Peace Delegation during the Vietnam War. Dr. Martin Luther King, Jr., nominated him for the Nobel Peace Prize. In one of his many books, *Being Peace*, Thich Nhat Hanh says, "We tend to be alive in the future, not now. We say, 'Wait until I finish school and get my Ph.D. degree, and then I will be really alive'... we are not capable of being alive in the present moment. We tend to postpone being alive to the future, the distant future, we don't know when. Now is not the moment to be alive. We may never be alive at all in our entire life. Therefore, the technique, if we have to speak of a technique, is to *be* in the present moment, to be aware that we are here and now, and the only moment to be alive is the present moment."

and feels new and alive. You can call this surrender and letting go. You can call it living in the now. A great many people throughout the world find this to be the essence of spirituality for them. Whatever you call it—and you don't have to call it anything at all—it feels sane, good, right, happy, and human. It is the root of being stress-free: relaxed, peaceful, and at ease.

When we learn to focus our attention completely in the present, we make an amazing discovery: problems we thought were huge begin to shrink, and old compulsions we thought we could never break out of fall away.

The problems of life are not really "out there"; they are "in here."

Excerpts from Eknath Easwaran, *Take Your Time: Finding Balance in a Hurried World*. New York: Hyperion, 1994.

ONE THING

In closing this segment, "The Real Deal Solution," I want to emphasize that these nine segments are all talking about one thing. They're just coming at it from different angles and words. But keep in mind that those segments are just a silly cutting up into slices of what is actually one thing. These nine segments are all describing one living, organic healing and growth process—one experience—that of feeling well, whole, peaceful, at ease in your skin and in your world. Remember that when the segments are not saying the exact same thing, they are at least deeply interconnected and overlapping.

For example, when your shame/image/esteem stuff starts to be brought into the light and air so it can heal, your overinvestment/attachment automatically lightens and your mind becomes more quiet more easily. On the other hand, someone who is truly committed to cultivating and trusting the quiet, silent mind will have access to the deep levels of wisdom, self-knowledge and healing that are inherent in that quiet mind. They will receive "messages" and insights from their deep inner wisdom, helping in the process of healing their shame/identity/image stuff. You get the idea.

Each one leads to the other, and they all lead to the same place: your own deep, inherent wholeness and happiness and peace. And that, as they say, is that. Find the angles in this segment that you dig and really get into them. Roll around in them. Read more about them. Ponder them. Digest them. Seek out people who live those angles that catch your attention. They will grow in you.

3 In The Meantime . . .

WHAT TO DO ABOUT YOUR STRESS WHILE YOU'RE LEARNING TO STOP CREATING IT

While you're there in the dead-center of the bull's eye, doing the real and gradual inner work of becoming radiantly peaceful, there are things you can and should do in the short term to get immediate relief. This third part is about ways to do that. Where part two was about not accumulating stress in the first place (that's why they're in the very center of the bull's eye), with this part, part three, we start to move to the outer circles. Now we take a brief look at all the things that help you *once the stress is already in you*. Even though they are not directly addressing the real causes of your stress, many of them are quite powerful. We'll start then, with the very first ring out, which includes "The Big Three" and "Nutritional Relationships." Just to repeat, the fact that I put these two in the first ring means that if you don't have the time, energy, or interest to attend to anything else in this third part of the book, attend to these. 'Nuff said.

Now we take a brief look at all the things that help you once the stress is already in you.

THE BIG THREE

If you really want to feel better quickly, do these three things: Eat well, start exercising, and get some good, sound rest. For most people, especially most Americans, these three things alone will make them feel reborn. Truly. Once the stress (fear, anxiety, etc.) is in you, these three: DIET, EXERCISE, & REST are the bottom line when it comes to quick relief and feeling a zillion times better.

Just about nobody in this world has anything even close to the obesity and chronic degenerative diseases that we have in America. Sometimes it seems as though we Americans eat as though we're partaking in a giant, nationwide race to see who can get heart disease or cancer first.

In the meantime, even if people don't succeed in creating an exotic and exciting disease, they do succeed in creating a body (and therefore a mind) which constantly swings between hyped-up, agitated overstimulation (sugar, caffeine, salt, etc.) and exhaustion. They often combat their exhaustion by cattle-prodding the body back into being "energized" with more sugar, caffeine, salt and so on. The cycle goes on until the body basically falls apart with diabetes, heart problems, or Lord knows what all. Everybody thinks this is normal because it's all they've ever known, and because it's how everyone they know lives.

We tend not to see commercials on TV telling people how they can essentially end all disease in their lives just by eating really well. This is because the produce department down at your local grocery store doesn't have the massive gazillions of dollars to advertise the benefits of plain, simple, healthy foods. The apples and grapes do not have high-powered lobbyists to influence public health and education agendas. And news media are interested in controversy and "hot copy," not actual sober education.

The treatment of disease, on the other hand, is a monolithic industry, involving massive billions upon billions of bucks. The entire medical and healthcare industry and the sprawling colossal health insurance industry and the monstrous pharmaceutical industry are not about to create a gigantic, prime-time advertising blitz, telling us: "People of America! You can put us all out of business by changing your lifestyle and radically changing your diet, which will essentially eliminate all need for us, ever, except for when you fall down stairs or skateboard into moving busses." Don't hold your breath waiting for this announcement. But that's another subject.

To create a dramatically more peaceful state of mind, try this, just as a temporary experiment: Knock all sugar, caffeine, and most salt out of your diet for a couple weeks or so. If you really want a leap into good, clear, shiny feeling, get rid of processed, refined carbohydrates, too—that's breads, muffins, pasta, everything made out of processed, refined flour. Of course, almost all of these foods (and I use the term loosely) have sugar and/or salt in them anyway, so if you were actually following the first dietary suggestion (dumping sugar, salt, and caffeine as a quick-relief experiment) that would get rid of most processed carbohydrates.

Now I've got to be honest with you, the first week or so may be sort of, well, nightmarishly unpleasant. These drug-like chemicals are addictive. You'll feel a whole lot worse, but then you'll feel a whole lot better, with a clarity, balance, and calmness you've never imagined. Of course, that's just a beginning, but it will serve as a powerful lesson in just how much your diet affects your mind, your thinking, and your moods.

In any case, whether you do that brave experiment or not, I believe that your first step is to *find out* about diet. Educate yourself. Learn a little bit.

Take that responsibility for your own health and well-being.

This is just a little bit un-American. In our country, we are often conditioned not to take responsibility for our own health, our own lives. Bad things that happen are somebody else's fault and there's always somebody who must be blamed and sued for the most inexplicable of life's accidents. And our health and well-being isn't our responsibility, it's the responsibility of the "authorities" and "experts" floating around "out there" somewhere, the medical establishment or the government or on TV or our mommies and daddies or Lord knows who else.

I would like you to begin to question and counter that whole notion. After all, it's your body. No one else's. I believe you should learn and know about it. Go against the current of our society. Read a book or two about diet. Listen to some audiotapes. Until you do, there's no vague notion of "what you should eat" that'll hold for long. You've

THE PROTEIN MYTH

There are many astonishing myths about diet in our country, myths that account for quite a lot of our health woes. One of them is a deeply misguided fixation on "getting enough protein." This fixation is largely the result of advertising and lobbying from the meat and dairy industries, starting in Germany at the turn of the century.

Today, modern research shows that we require dramatically less protein (20–35 grams for men or nonpregnant women) than has previously been propagated. *The Journal of Clinical Nutrition* states that we need about 2.5 percent of our total calories to be protein (roughly 18 grams of protein per day).

The American Dietetic Association says that pure vegetarian diets in America typically have twice the necessary protein for our daily requirements. Harvard researchers have shown that it is very hard for a vegetarian diet to produce a protein deficiency unless excessive junk foods and sweets are being consumed. The Max Planck Institute has shown that superior complete proteins are found in numerous plant-based sources, including almonds, sesame seeds, pumpkinseeds, sunflower seeds, soybeans, buckwheat, peanuts, potatoes, all leafy greens, and most fruits. Many fruits have the same percentage of complete protein as mother's milk.

Finally, tons of research out there links high protein diets (like that of the average, meat-eating American) to diseases such as arthritis, pyorrhea, schizophrenia, atherosclerosis, heart disease, cancer, kidney damage, premature aging, overall tissue, organ and cell degeneration, toxic bacterial growth in the colon, deficiencies of B6 and B3, hypertension, and adult-onset diabetes. Excess protein has also been found to leach out calcium, iron, zinc, and magnesium from our bodies. As Gabriel Cousens, M.D. states in his master work, *Conscious Eating,* "The evidence is overwhelming that the most important single dietary change one can make to prevent osteoporosis is to decrease the amount of protein in the diet . . . female vegetarians [have] five times less bone loss than nonvegetarian women."

got to have at least a basic idea of how and why. Find out what all the nasty, poison glop we put into our bodies actually does to us, to our liver, our kidneys, and our endocrine system. In specific, gory, gruesome detail.

Where you'll end up, of course, is (duh!) eating lots more fresh, organic raw fruits and vegetables, and fresh, organic, raw nuts and seeds. Sometimes even whole meals of the stuff. The way every other biological organism on the planet eats (in their natural environment.) Real, actual food. Full of living enzymes and life force and perfectly balanced blends of vitamins, minerals, fats, and proteins. The way nature made 'em.

You know all those zillions of books about different diets? After a lifetime of study, here's what I believe is as complicated a system as you really need:

1. Fruits, veggies, nuts, seeds—very, very good (nuts and raw seeds, maybe soaked overnight in water—makes them much more digestible; fruits and veggies, fresh, raw, as much as possible. Giant salads and so on, though lightly steamed veggies are fine). Eat as many as you can.

2. Whole grains and legumes—still pretty darn good. By grains I mean stuff like oats, brown rice, buckwheat, millet, barley, quinoa (not processed and refined, like in commercial breakfast cereals. The actual whole, un-messed-with grain).

3. Dairy—not good. See John Robbins' books in bibiography.

4. Meat—in general, pretty darn bad. Red meat is quite bad. Ditto pork. Poultry and fish, in moderation, if they're not laden with chemicals, hormones, antibiotics, mercury, and other toxins and neurotoxins, are okay.

5. Everything else—bad. This includes all processed, refined, prepackaged "foods," convenience foods, "ready-to-eat" foods, snack foods and so on.

6. Sugar, salt, caffeine, fried fats/heated oils—spectacularly bad. (We'll talk about drugs like alcohol and nicotine later.)

There. Isn't that easy? Paste that on your refrigerator. Or your forehead. These are not suggested as rigid rules, but rather as rough, general guidelines. Just tack very gradually, very patiently in this dietary direction. Give yourself a few years if you need to, but, little by little, you'll start to feel almost reborn. While you educate yourself about this stuff, you may also need to educate your parents a little too. They'll thank you some day. For your education, some authors who are not just "flash in the pan" faddists but real heavyweights are Bernard Jensen, Paavo Airola, Gabriel Cousens, and Jeffery Bland.

If you even come close to the sort of transformative diet I'm talking about, your stress level will be cut at least in half. Other little fringe benefits include incredible energy, clear eyes, great skin, healthy and perfect hair, good breath, all kinds of weight loss, and the avoidance of countless disgusting and gruesome diseases.

My advice on exercise? Do so. These bodies of ours were designed to move about. So move about. Every day. The ideal? Swim. Do yoga. Lift some weights (NOT excessively). These, to me, are the three finest forms of exercise for your body and mind. Some combination of them will give you the most vigorous, balanced, enduring health that exercise can provide. Swimming tones, strengthens, and works your cardiovascular system, while being totally easy on your joints. Yoga decompresses, opens, lengthens, and strengthens your body like nothing else in the world!

Whereas gravity and emotional stress and improper body use are always contracting your body and compressing joints and shortening tissues and pulling you out of alignment, yoga opens and aligns joints, lengthens your body, brings mobility and stability. It rocks. While yoga *is* resistance training, a bit of weight training is an excellent thing, too. It strengthens ligaments and bones and muscles and tendons, makes you resilient to injury and even improves your immune system, just for good measure.

But if you can't do, or can't stand those three, almost any exercise (done smartly) is better than none. Jogging, fast walking, bicycle riding, dancing, wrestling, gymnastics, team sports, rock climbing, martial arts, fencing, rollerblading, tennis, whatever!

Here's the deal. Or at least a deal: for several million years (give or take an epoch) of our evolution, stress came from a direct threat of some sort, say a giant, crazed, prehistoric woodchuck leaping out of the bush. Then zappo, the "stress response" would get triggered in the body. This is also called

the "fight or flight" response, where the adrenal glands (among others) suddenly shoot the body full of stress chemicals (stress hormones) that enable us to react with accelerated speed and power and not feel pain as much. Then, that big "charge" of energy got totally discharged by the vigorous action of either fighting or fleeing

(running the heck away.) But in the last few thousand years (give or take an aeon) the threats that stress us out have gotten less and less direct and immediate. They've gotten more abstract and removed, less and less like giant, crazed, prehistoric woodchucks leaping out from bushes.

Nowadays, they're these omnipresent, free-floating amorphous threats, hovering out there somewhere: What will happen if my grades stink? How will things ever get okay with my nutty parents? What if my boyfriend fools around with that evily beautiful nymphet in his math class? What if my life is a stupid failure? Oy!! It's enough to make you long for the occasional giant, crazed, prehistoric woodchuck! The amorphous, abstract "threats" of modern life never go away—at least not all of them. So we suffer a constant, low-grade "fight or flight" response in our bodies 24/7 instead of one-time events that happen and then are over.

So with these abstract, modern "threats" there is no immediate, present, real action to take that will *discharge* all that stress energy and chemistry from the body. It just builds up and makes us miserable and sick.

Exercise discharges that stimulation and "excitation" in the sympathetic nervous system. It releases the stress chemistry in the body so that, to the body, it's something like having just successfully fought—or escaped from—the giant, crazed, prehistoric woodchuck. The short way to say all this is just to point to what most people have already experienced: exercise makes you feel much, much better. If you're stressed out, then it *really* makes you feel better.

So take the time and energy to really look into the matter and find a form of exercise that you enjoy. Most people say that even three or four times a week of exercise that gets you out of breath and a bit sweaty for 20–30 minutes is enough, though every day would be recommended for those who feel really stressed and for those who are really serious about getting unstressed.

Two other points about exercise. Variety is really excellent. Our bodies—not to mention our minds—were not meant for endless mechanical repetition of the same movement patterns and rhythms. Swim one day, take a long, brisk walk the next, play some basketball the next, lift some weights, and play some baseball the next.

The third of our big three is, of course, rest. You need sleep and plenty of it. Because compulsive, addictive, frantic busyness is the insane "American way,"

most Americans are, by medical definition, sleep-deprived.

Allow me to remind you that sleep deprivation is used as a means of torture. Sleep-deprived people are crabby and snappy, they can't think clearly, their attention span sucks and, worst of all, the brain chemicals that make us sane and happy get all messed up. Oh yeah, sleep-deprived people are also sleepy and have low energy. But I guess you probably knew that.

It is very stressful to be low on sleep. Some suggestions for a good night's sleep are: to go to bed at the same time every night, and not do stimulating, excitatory activities in the last hour or two before you turn in for sleep. Do mellow, sedating things. Take a bath. Don't watch TV—we'll

talk about that later. Read something fairly chilled out,
something that won't get you all worked up. Then head to
sleep, and not on a full stomach. Sweet dreams.

NUTRITIOUS RELATIONSHIPS

Once that stress is already in you (and again, this whole
section is all about "once that stress in already in you") one
of the very best most powerful ways you can feel good and
happy again is to talk openly to a good, caring friend.

    We are social, communal creatures. There's a part of us
(a not very happy part) that hates that fact; hates the vul-
nerability of it. But connecting, bonding with others is absolutely crucial to our health and sanity, no
two ways about it. In AA they say "We're
only as sick as our secrets." Because sharing
painful things with others makes those
painful things lose their power. They shift
and change when we bring them out into the
light of day. The stuck energy of that pain
and the whole pattern breaks up and moves.
Most of us have had that experience of talking to a good friend and then somehow feeling like our burdens were lighter; everything
felt somehow different. Somehow better.

    Unfortunately, teenagers are also notorious
for making spectacularly awful decisions
about who they choose as friends and also for
accepting way too much toxic psychic glop
from these people. So *you've* got to take responsibility to make sure that you have at least one friend
who is truly respectful and caring; who really accepts you
for who you are, exactly as you are. Not that there's nothing whatsoever about you that bugs them; everyone has
traits that bug people. But in general, that they dig you;
they essentially love who you are and want what's best for
you and they also challenge you to grow. Even when you're
driving 'em crazy—and all friends drive each other crazy
now and then. They would never abuse you or treat you

DID YOU KNOW?

"Many researchers now believe that
the symptom most common among
those vulnerable to stress is emotional isolation."

    The same article quotes Jonathan
Schedler, a research psychologist
affiliated with Harvard University:
"The fact is humans are emotionally
frail. We need real support from other
people, and those who don't acknowl-
edge it are going to feel besieged."

**Excerpts from B. Carey, "Don't Face
Stress Alone."** *Health Magazine*
(April 1997): p. 78.

disrespectfully. It feels good to be around them and you trust them.

If you have one of these friends already, you are lucky. Learn to talk to them about your deepest pain. Not just cheap complaining. But really opening up to them. If you don't have such a friend, start to consciously hold the intention that you want one (at least one) and that you deserve that. Exude that deservingness and that intention. Create the space for it, in your willingness, and put some energy out into the world, in terms of actually going out and doing stuff where you can meet people. Be interested in people and genuinely open yourself. It'll happen.

CHANGING YOUR ACTIVITIES: DOING LESS, SAYING NO, DOING NOTHING, HAVING FUN

Before we talk about altering your activities, I have to emphasize that, since stress does come from the inside out (have I mentioned that?)

you absolutely do not have to be doing lots of busy stuff to feel stressed-out.

Many, many people feel totally stressed and overwhelmed who really don't do much at all. As a matter of fact, that stress—caused by their thinking, their identity, all the stuff we spoke about in part two of this book—is often what keeps people from doing things, even while it increases their sense of pressure for not doing them! Stress can be paralyzing and is always exhausting.

So, if that's you, stressed-out but not busy, please understand how normal it is.

It doesn't mean your stress and pain are any less "real" than super-busy people.

Maybe this bit on doing less, saying no, doing nothing and having fun doesn't apply so much to you. I'd suggest you check it out anyway though. You'll probably still find some useful things in it. Plus, you never know; it might apply to you a little more than you think it does. Here we go.

QUOTE FROM CHRISTIAN KOMOR

I know many obsessive-compulsives who do not work long hours. I know many workaholics who do not appear to be over-achievers.

Excerpt from Christian Komor, *The Power of Being: For People Who Do Too Much!* Grand Rapids, Mich.: Renegade House Productions, 1991.

Doing Less

Stressed-out, busy, frantic types have the most elaborate, the most passionately defended reasons why they simply "*can't*" do less. They believe in these reasons with a religious intensity. They'll tell you all about how, "if I don't write for the school paper then I won't get the summer internship at the weekly, and if I don't get the summer internship at the weekly I won't get into the highly selective journalism program at NYU, and if I don't get into that journalism program, I'll end up a disease-ridden bag lady eating gum wrappers and if I end up a disease-ridden bag lady eating gum wrappers all life on earth as we know it will end and the universe will implode into a black hole."

Stressed-out people have all got one of these stories. What's worse, they've got one such story for every single thing they're doing in their lives. There's always some terrible sequence of disastrous events, as sure as a row of falling dominoes, that'll happen if they cut back on some activities.

It's all sillyness. If this is you, you've simply got to learn to do less. Concretely. Practically. Literally. Do less. Hack things away. To alter one of Nike's slogans: *Just don't do it.* For example, if you're not deeply, passionately in love with soccer, and you feel stressed-out in your life, quit the soccer team with its ten hours a week of practice! (Instead, just do four or five 30-minute workouts a week.) You just saved yourself 7½ hours a week.

Spend those 7½ hours in a hammock with a lemonade.

In a clear, relaxed, quiet moment, take a hard look at your life. Write out roughly how many hours you spend each week doing what. Better yet, keep track of what you do, of how you spend your time, for one solid week, or even a month. Write it down. Carry a little notepad with you. This exercise never fails to amaze and shock people.

Many awarenesses of ways to "do less" will come to you just from doing this exercise. But one thing you should definitely do is to pick out those things you do just because "you should." Because people say you should or because "everybody else does." Quit those. Disappoint some people. They'll live. So will you. No, I'm not talking about the basics of getting along in the world, like school, for instance. That would actually be much, much more stressful in the long run. But all those "extras" that we all tend to get ourselves into.

This doing too much extra stuff, over and above what you really, truly have to do, can come from two places. One I just mentioned: a sense of wanting to please or impress someone or other, wanting to avoid disappointing them or to fulfill someone's wacky expectations of you. The other is just really wanting to do tons of things. This one is the trickiest.

What you'll need to learn is that even neat, cool things that you really want to do can easily—and swiftly—turn into your enemies. Here's how it works: You're in a phase where you're feeling great, full of enthusiasm and brimming over with energy. In this mood, you exuberantly sign up for an evening class and you start a band and you tell your little brother you'll help him with his morning paper route before school. What you fail to realize is that moods come in cycles, in phases, and that the buoyant, dynamic mood of this week will be followed by moods of tiredness and heaviness. It's as certain and dependable as the seasons.

In those moods, you will feel like the *victim* of these new involvements and projects. Suddenly there are all these deadlines, obligations, time demands and people counting on you. You discover that it's often way easier to get into new activities and commitments than to get out of them. And the real, day-to-day work of the involvement turns out to be different, more homely, than the enthusiastic mental images that swam in your head when you first "signed up." You find out that you only have so much "juice," or emotional energy with which to pursue projects *and* stay sane, healthy, and effective.

By the time I was in my late teens, I had exuberantly plunged into writing, acting, music, (playing guitar in a rock band), martial arts, and Zen Buddhist Training. I loved each of these in their own unique way and couldn't imagine giving up any of them. But after a few years of juggling all of these activities, the weariness and time demands started to catch up to me and I slowly realized that I had to make some hard choices. First I cut out the music, then about six months later the acting, and finally, several years later, I hacked away the martial arts. All of these were painful decisions. But not only was my life simplified and made more balanced by these decisions, but by focusing on just two pursuits (writing and Zen practice) I was able to go into those two with much more depth. In other words, I was able to put many hours per week into two things, instead of just a few hours per week into five things.

—*Mark Powell*

But I wasn't just talking nonsense when I said you should do this reassessment of your life involvements from a clear, peaceful state of mind. This is actually pretty important. One of the sure traits of a racing, busy, stressed-out mind is a major lack of perspective. You're like a different person, one who cannot see the big picture or think clearly. Your I.Q. literally goes way down when you're stressed-out.

Lastly, keep in mind that if you're a super busy "do-a-holic," you probably get all sorts of praise for your craziness. Compulsive, addictive, health-destroying "doing" and busyness is the "norm" for our crazy culture. People might say you are "Dynamic!" They beam at you with approval and admiration. It will require a staggering amount of strength, intelligence, and self-possession to recognize all of that as patent insanity. It will require courage and self-respect to walk away from it, and to choose your own path, the path of serenity and relaxation, instead of being a dancing bear for other people's neurotic expectations.

Feel compassion for these folks adoring you for your manic busyness: they're a little nuts and they don't know it. They mean well. What *you* are involved in, what *you* are learning about, is the peace, relaxation and looseness that will allow you to fully, deeply live and enjoy your life—not frantically race through it—and that allows you much *greater* effectiveness and productivity in your life pursuits. It is not easy to step away from the crowd, the hypnotic trance of the frantic, scrambling mob. But—at least to some degree—you must if radiant inner peace is your goal.

Saying No

A very important part of doing less is the fine art of saying "no" to people. This is a very powerful and empowering thing to do. It's an affirmation of strength, of boundaries, and of who you are. It is a placing of limits. And saying "no" to people is taking a stand for your values and priorities; what you're all about.

It says to the world that your time is important; a valuable commodity (and by the way, people will gladly take all of it from you if you let them). It also says to the world that you're strong enough in yourself; that you're not driven to please other people. It says that you know life is about choices: you can't do everything or please everyone and you must take care of your own mental and physical health first, or you'll have nothing to give to the world, so you make choices. To choose or say "yes" to one thing is, simultaneously, to unchoose, or say no, to countless others.

Many of the things you must learn to say "no" to are obvious things: projects that don't serve your heart's desire and your well-being, too many favors, and so on. "Hey, will you help organize the party? You want to work on the school paper?" Don't respond to such invitations right away. **Learn to take some time to reflect before taking on a new involvement. Start becoming deeply sensitive and honest within yourself and finding out: Are these things right for you? Can you really do this, in terms of time and energy? If not, the answer is: No. No. And no.**

But really, most of the important no's, and probably the hardest ones, are social. Begin to notice if you frequently end up doing things with people who don't contribute to your aliveness; things which, afterward, leave you feeling scattered, drained, empty, or otherwise not good. These are the sorts of people and activities to start saying "no" to. It's one thing to have some real "quality time" with a friend or a group of friends, where you're truly present and connected with them and your soul feels nourished afterward. It's another thing entirely to just "hang out" for hours, not really having fun, not really connected to the person or people you're with. You must learn that your time is worth much more than that. *You're* worth much more than that. Start saying "no" to more and more of these things. Let the people you're saying "no" to have their feelings. They'll survive. It's part of life.

Doing Nothing

Doing nothing is a long lost art that you should cultivate. Your guilt and uptightness might make it hard; it might

QUOTE FROM CHRISTIAN KOMOR

When we "do nothing" we are actually doing something very important! We are shifting from doing to being. This eventually brings us back to ourselves, which is what we've been missing all along.

Excerpt from Christian Komor, *The Power of Being: For People Who Do Too Much!* Grand Rapids, Mich.: Renegade House Productions, 1991 drive you to start doing something, anything. It'll make you miserable. That's okay. Be miserable. And continue with your doing nothing. Look at it like an alcoholic going through withdrawal. (It's not all that far from the truth of the matter, because we actually do become addicted to the intensity and adrenalin of a frantic lifestyle.) And if you feel guilty for not "doing" things, just sit there and feel guilty. You'll survive.

Lay on a beach or on the grass. Watch the clouds. Watch the trees move in the tall breezes. Listen to birds. Sit on a park bench. Stare at a mountain or brook. Sit and people-watch at a mall. Lay by your dog or cat and just pet him or her. Chew on a long blade of grass. Lay in a hammock. Sit in front of a fire and gaze into the flames. Take a slow, ambling, drifting, aimless walk. Watch snow fall. Sit quietly and just breathe.

Of course, strictly speaking, these things aren't "nothing," but they approximate "nothing" in the sense that they are not about "achieving" or "accomplishing" anything in particular. This is very healthy for us human types. "Purposeless being" is like a de-compression chamber for your brain. Necessary for sanity. (As you'll read shortly, TV definitely does NOT count!)

Now, yeah, yeah, yeah, I know: us wacky compulsive "do-a-holic" types will invariably approach "doing nothing" in the same compulsive "doing" way that we do everything else. "I'm busily accomplishing this stress-reducing activity." The solution? Sheer quantity. Sooner or later, for many people, after enough guilty, fretful, miserable fidgeting, you'll hit a wall and your mind will start to quiet down a little. Find out if you're one of those many. If you're not, and your mind never settles down and it stays tortured, do it anyway. It's still good for you. You'll get better at it with time, and if you work with other ideas in this book.

Having Fun

Along with doing nothing comes the business of doing fun stuff; recreation, play, and creativity. Stressed-out people usually don't do enough fun stuff, and even when they do, they're often still stressed-out even while they do them. (Why? Say it along with me: Stress comes from how we think, not from what we do or don't do!) All the things they "should be doing" still hang over their heads.

What to do? It's essentially the "doing nothing" advice: being very honest with yourself, *know* that you have this "stress-mind" habit and do the fun stuff anyway. You want to get to the point of self-knowledge and self-honesty where you can gently say to yourself, "of course I'm still stressed-out, even at this party/dance/bowling alley/concert/beach; I have a long-ingrained mental habit that is gonna take time to grow out of." The only time you'll really get into trouble is when you try to kid yourself, denial style. Instead, humbly know where you're at; be straight and real with yourself about it, and throw yourself compassionately into fun, leisure, recreation, and play.

So spend some time making a list of recreation that attracts you. Parties, dances, playing cards, bowling, taking walks, camping or hiking, shooting baskets, reading silly novels, knitting or sewing, performing exorcisms, cooking, time travel, whatever. Don't wait for "free time" in which to do them. Make the time. Schedule these things in. They're vital to your health and sanity.

COMMON SENSE: SMOKING, DRUGS, AND TV

For some people this category (smoking, drugs, TV) will be more primary than for others. It depends on the person

Bodies full of toxins always have wacky mood swings.

(keeping in mind that, as I said earlier in this book, actual drug/alcohol addiction is far beyond the scope of this book. Those addictions—and other issues, like eating disorders—are serious, life-and-death matters requiring professional intervention. The drug/alcohol use I'm talking about here is the so-called "casual use/abuse" that is common among teenagers, but that doesn't show the *specific* hallmarks of addiction).

But either way, if you are truly sick and tired of feeling stressed-out, you'll take a serious look at smoking, drugs (including alcohol) and TV. If you don't indulge in these profoundly unwise habits you have my permission to skip this segment. Otherwise, read on.

If you smoke or do drugs (by the way, anytime I refer to drugs, I'm including alcohol in there, too, okay?) you'd probably swear that these things relax you, right? Here's why they don't.

You may recall that

"stress" is just a newfangled word for oldfangled emotions, especially fear, but also anger and guilt.

If you think about it for a moment you'll see that when you're stressed, you are scared, angry, whatever at specific things, inside you and/or outside you. To experience actual peace and release, you need to change things, in how you perceive and think or in outer action, or both. Smoking, drugs, and TV do neither. They do worse than neither because they numb and anesthetize you. Here are some of the problems with numbing and anesthetizing your painful emotions (aka, stress).

1. The real causes of your stress stay totally unchanged (if you're wildly honest with yourself, you have to confess that even while numbed up real good you still aren't truly, deeply, loose, at ease, expansive).

2. The things making you feel stressed actually get worse when you ignore and suppress them. Troubles

and conflicts in our psychology are like that; they build up and get more extreme when ignored or suppressed. Think of the things actually causing your stress (within and seemingly without) as a fire in your house or apartment building. The smoke alarm going off is your stress and discomfort. Drugs, cigarettes, and TV are like cutting the wires to the smoke alarm and thinking you've solved the problem because you've stopped that loud, obnoxious sound. There's still this little issue of the fire, and it gets worse the longer you ignore it.

3. You actually get worse and worse at handling the actual causes of your stress because each time you turn to smoking, drugs, and/or TV you subconsciously send yourself a strong, clear message: "I can't handle life. I can't handle my emotions. I'm too small, weak, and incapable." Of course in reality you're nothing of the kind, no matter how good you've gotten at fooling yourself and others that you are. The more you tell yourself these lies, not only do you start to believe them, but you also start to lose all respect for yourself. Yuck.

DID YOU KNOW?

In his superb book, *Evolution's End*, Joseph Chilton Pearce talks about research that's been done on how watching TV affects the brain. Apparently, the part of the brain that's all about imagining, creating, and envisioning shows all sorts of activity if we're reading, writing, listening to a story, pretty much if we're doing anything—except watching TV. With TV, that part of the brain "flatlines;" that is, it's dormant, dead, nothing going on, zero activity. But the really bad part is that there's only a small window of time, as we grow up, when that part of the brain (the imagining, creating, and envisioning part) can develop. If it doesn't develop then, it never will. When kids watch a lot of TV, that function of the brain atrophies—it withers away—never to develop. The hypothesis then, is that many teenagers who experience a lot of despair and hopelessness feel that way because they never acquired the ability to imagine and envision more for themselves, more for their lives, more for the world. Because they could not envision, period.

You should also be very clear that these things actually end up stressing you out more, not less. Drugs and cigs toxify your body in a major way. Your metabolism revs to purge the toxins from your body, your vitality drops, you get mood and energy swings.

Drugs and cigs feel good in the moment, but they're actually making the stress much worse and making you less able to undo that stress. So you need more and more to get the same result.

Think of it this way: By indulging in drugs and cigarettes today, you're buying tomorrow's (or next week's, whatever) stressed-out, depressed mood. Then, by indulging in drugs and/or cigarettes to medicate tomorrow's stressed-out, depressed mood, you're making an even bigger "deposit" toward the next day's even worse stressed-out, depressed mood. And so on.

As for TV, there are many reasons people used to call TV the "idiot box." They should also call it the "stress box."

TV should be called the "stressed-out idiot box."

If you don't watch in moderation, TV has the same "numb-out-and-suppress-uncomfortable-emotions" effect as drugs and smoking. But TV, though it doesn't toxify you chemically, makes you mentally agitated and jittery by the totally unnatural pace and rhythm of what we watch; blankly staring at the flashing of images every couple of seconds creates disturbed, erratic brainwave patterns in people. That's not how life looks, works, or feels, nor how we were designed to perceive and relate to life. So even though it seems to somehow distract us from our troubles, it simultaneously makes us nervous and uptight. (Incidentally, for those interested, TV actually does a lot more nasty stuff to us than I've mentioned here. Check out a book called *Evolution's End*, by Joseph Chilton Pearce.) In any case, the wisest course, when it comes to TV, is to pick a couple of shows that you really, really adore and watch only those. Dump the rest. Be happy.

MORE ON TV

In his book, *Four Arguments for the Elimination of Television*, Jerry Mander says, "when you are a watching, absorbing technoguru, your mind . . . is certainly not 'empty mind.' Images are pouring into it. Your mind is not quiet or calm or empty. It may be nearer to dead or zombie-ized. It is occupied. No renewal can come from this condition. For renewal, the mind would have to be at rest, or once rested, it would have to be seeking new kinds of stimulation, new exercise. Television offers neither rest nor stimulation.

"Television inhibits your ability to think, but it does not lead to freedom of mind, relaxation or renewal. It leads to a more exhausted mind. . . . The mind is never empty, the mind is filled. What's worse, it is filled with someone else's obsessive thoughts and images."

Zoiks!

PROCRASTINATION

Here's another obvious one yet somehow, many of us miss it entirely. (It's called "not seeing the forest for all of the trees.") It's this: feeling anxious and stressed without ever really, consciously realizing that the reason you feel that way is because you're procrastinating horribly on work you should be handling! This is like wondering why you feel uncomfortable while somehow not noticing the elephant standing on your toe. In this instance, your stressful feelings are trying to tell you something: Handle business! Stop procrastinating and get to work! You'll feel better. Lots better.

I think most people would do well to read one or two good books on procrastination. Procrastination is stressful as all get out; it hurts, it makes us miserable, and it can wreck people's lives. Truly! So look at a book or two. It's worth your trouble. Don't put it off.

But in the meantime, here are a couple of basic points without delving into the psychology of procrastination (fear of failure, etc.)

1. What most people really fear is not the work, it's actually just *starting* the work. To start with, on your first day, promise yourself that you're only going to *begin* whatever it is you have to do. That's it. Fifteen minutes or something like that. Guarantee yourself that you won't go past that on this day.

2. Cut the project up into small, manageable slices, and just do one a day—or 20 minutes a day, an hour every other day, whatever seems doable.

3. Make sure you end your day's work at a place that's easy for you to pick up again tomorrow; at a place where you know exactly what your next (tomorrow's) step is going to be. Try to almost never stop at a tricky, intimidating point—it'll be much harder to pick it up again tomorrow (or whatever). This is a Hemingway trick. He would only stop writing on any given day at a point where he knew exactly where the story was going next.

4. Come up with small rewards that you can "earn" and give yourself for accomplishing your work—whatever you really enjoy—shooting some baskets, reading a fun magazine in a hot bath, laying at a beach. If you can afford it, even buy yourself a CD, or a book, or go to a movie. Come up with larger rewards for when you've completely finished a project or chunk of work: a whole day at the beach or whatever.

The tricky thing is that even super-busy people who are running around stressfully doing all sorts of stuff are very often not "handling business." It looks to you or me like "handling business" is *all* they do, but in fact they're crazy-busy with the WRONG STUFF! Their minds are so busy and cluttered and racing that they get their priorities all mixed up. Hence, all their frenetic busyness actually turns out to be a form of avoiding the things they REALLY should be doing, usually because, deep down (or not so deep down) they're really scared that they can't handle the tasks they should be doing.

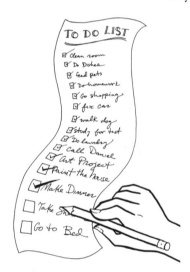

By the way, when I say "should," I'm not *just* talking about the "shoulds" that come from "out there"—school, coaches, obligations, and so on. I'm also talking about things your heart tells you that you should be doing to live the life you most deeply yearn to live. Like, maybe your heart yearns to be a poet and to be true to yourself you know you have to work at it regularly. But you don't. You allow life's obligations and busyness and involvements to "put off" your poetry writing. This also is procrastination. Although your deepest self longs to write poetry, there are more superficial parts of you that are insecure, scared to try, scared you won't be able to do it. So you put it off. Part of changing this is psychological. Facing these fears and moving through them would unfortunately require a whole book of its own (though part two of this book can give a lot of indications). But another part is very concrete, which brings us to our next chapter.

TIME MANAGEMENT

If there's one phrase I hate more than "stress reduction" it's "time management," and here I am forced, forced, I tell you, to get redundant: as George Pransky says, the very fact that someone is interested in "time management" shows, without a doubt, that his or her *mind* is way too busy and cluttered, his or her thoughts racing. The quiet mind is not in the least need of "time management" anything! Time manages itself, effortlessly! That said, since, as we discussed, cultivating the quiet mind takes time, I will say just this much: Priorities. You need 'em. They're your friend. You gotta know, clearly within you, what are the most important things to be attending to and what are less important. Then you can schedule your day a little.

Ultimately we're all unique and we all must create our own way of working with priorities and scheduling: what works for me may not work for you. Stephen Covey has some excellent wisdom on this point. He says there's a difference between the urgent and the important (though he may use different words). "The important" are things like our poetry example, things you must build and create to be true to yourself, to your vision, to your spiritual well-being; to honor the life and gifts you've been given, to contribute to the world, to nurture your spirit. "The urgent" are things like studying for some hateful test, practicing for the basketball game, typing up your resume for a job. The tendency, and the error most people make, is they let the urgent put off the important. Forever. But what is the point of a life that's only the urgent? It's life as a "get the list done" machine.

The trick is to balance the urgent, the important, and everything in between.

DID YOU KNOW?

Dr. Stephen R. Covey is an internationally respected leadership authority and organizational consultant, among other things. (Lots of them.) In other words, gigantic corporations all over the world pay him gigantic bucks to advise them on how to get their act together.

Covey wrote this book called *The 7 Habits of Highly Effective People*, which sold a few gazillion copies in 32 languages and 75 countries. It's a major modern-day classic in the arena of books on getting your act together, prioritizing, finding satisfaction in achieving your goals, and being effective. Dr. Covey calls his approach "Principle-Centered Living" (and "Principle-Centered Leadership").

The important is just as high a priority as the urgent. Know this and create your priority list wisely and beautifully. Actually write it out. Then write a third list, the self-care list. These are things that are necessary to take care of yourself, physically, emotionally, and spiritually. Exercise, naps, long walks, all the stuff we've talked about in this book. Because one amazingly vital point about priorities is that no matter how urgent some life imperative appears, it is not worth your mental, emotional, and/or physical health.

Your health and well-being must come first, or you'll have nothing to give anyone else, and no juice left to create the things you want to create in your life.

Sick, exhausted, frazzled people do not contribute to the world. They drain it. So have your priority list, including the urgent, the important and the self-care. Then with that in front of you, take a separate piece of paper and make your schedule for the day or week. Try one day at a time (tomorrow). A whole week "scheduled" seems unrealistic to me. But everyone's different. Experiment and find what works for you.

Creating this balance of the urgent, the important, and self-care stuff in your priority lists is a forever ongoing "work in progress." It's a fluid, ever-changing matter; you never "get it perfect" (which is a stress-creating notion anyway). So don't get uptight about it. You always adapt, modulate, and alter as each space and slice of time goes on and as you change. Have fun with these priority lists. Play with them, tinker with them. And promise yourself that you won't beat up on yourself for not sticking to your schedule. Almost no one sticks to his or her schedules perfectly and people who do are often a little scary. It's just a rough guide to shoot for and provide a general structure to create the life you want. Most of all though, you'll find that, as the inner work we looked at (in part two of this book) progresses in you, the whole picture of your priorities and your time use will effortlessly become clear, simple, and obvious to you. It will be natural.

DAILY ROUTINE AND ORDER IN YOUR SURROUNDINGS

Two things that add all kinds of really unnecessary stress are:

1. A chaotic way of careening through your day.
2. Chaotic and cluttered living spaces.

Now I know teenagers are notorious for both of these things. If the teenage me could've looked into the future and seen present-day me writing this he would have ruptured many organs, so hard would he have laughed. So I'm not hoping for crazy miracles here, but even tiny improvements in these two areas can really help us feel a lot more calm, clear, and sane.

If you're the kind of person who sort of careens erratically through your day, try to build in even the most meager routines. Like wake up, brush teeth, shower, do a few minutes of stretching, then sit for ten minutes and reflect on the kind of day you want (i.e., calm, centered) or, just before bed, always brush your teeth, pick up your room a little bit, then read for a little bit in bed before you go to sleep. Create little rituals that you do every day, like coming home from school, having a little snack, then laying quietly to shift gears out of "school gear." Start to build some structure into your day. Of course some stressed-out people are overly structured already. To the point of rigidity and tight control. This feels yucky. If that's you, ignore this whole part. Loosen up, okay?

Most people have experienced how much clearer their minds feel when they've really cleaned up and organized their living space. Notice this. If you have time (and it doesn't stress you out more) make use of this to help yourself; to give yourself a bit more clarity and space in your mind.

The POM folks are quick to point out that a person who's learned to live in the natural way—i.e., with a quiet mind—experiences an effortless, flowing structure in her day and a natural order in her living environment. True indeed. But again, until we're there or during those times in which we can't slow our minds down to save our lives, doing it backward helps. That is to say, a quiet mind results in an ordered day and home, but an ordered day and home can also sometimes contribute toward a quiet mind.

CREATIVITY

For many people—of any age—a creative outlet helps them to transform stress or even to work through some of the emotional issues causing it. Creative endeavors are also therapeutic because you forget about yourself when ab-

sorbed in your art. It can be an activity, then, that re-establishes you in that totally carefree, abandoned, timeless state that very young children are in while they build or create something. And *that* is very, very good for you. It washes away stress.

So, either begin to cultivate, or get more deeply into whatever grabs you: writing, visual arts, music, photography, filmmaking, gardening, woodworking, dance, animation, sculpture. If it makes you happy (even in a maddening, struggling-with-this-or-that-aspect of your art way) do it and do it a lot. There's more than one person who wouldn't have made it to adulthood without his or her art.

SOLITUDE

This idea of solitude may seem to go against the chapter about nutritious relationships, but we humans also require some solitude now and again, and some of us require more than others. See if you can find a place, out in nature if possible, where you can just sort of commune with yourself, a place to hang out alone and be with your thoughts and feelings. A park, a lake, a library. Sometimes, when we're super stressed-out, one of the only things that'll really help is to find some way to go on a little "retreat" of some kind.

This may not be practical for a lot of teenagers, but there are frequently religious places, monasteries, retreat centers, and so on where you can go on a retreat, usually pretty cheaply—even if you're not religious. If you don't drive, of course, you'll need to arrange for some form of transportation or use public transport if it's safe. But even two days, a weekend of quiet solitude—though it may sound like torture— can totally revolutionize your mind-set and give you some perspective on your situation.

If your parents are especially generous, maybe they'll pay for you to spend a couple nights at a hotel. Get creative about it. The best of all is if you can arrange for a couple days of solitary camping. You might be able to talk your parents into this if it's a tame, well-maintained, not-too-remote campground with other campsites and people nearby.

Of course, I always have caveats for each chapter. Here's this one: Remember the chapter where I said that we humans are social, communal creatures and need lots of healthy intimacy and connection with our fellow humans? Well, this is very true, so if you're already way into being alone, you probably do *not* need more of it.

With a lot of people, maybe most, their problem is that they don't have enough nutritious closeness with people. This is *not* the same as solitude; it's something very different called isolation.

Solitude can be healthy. Isolation is never healthy. And solitude is only good for you if you're coming from a foundation of some decent genuine emotional closeness with people. If you feel humanly isolated, or even suspect you may be, solitude is not what you need. But if you have some nurturing friendships in your life, then solitude can be a beautiful, calming, centering, healing way to get to know yourself and wash away stress. It can make you sane again.

@@@@@@@@@

ONE EXCELLENT BREATHING TECHNIQUE TO DE-STRESS

"The single most effective relaxation technique I know is conscious regulation of breath. . . . To learn it I suggest you do it seated with your back straight. Place the tip of your tongue against the ridge of tissue just behind your upper front teeth, and keep it there through the entire exercise.

▶ First exhale completely through your mouth, making a whoosh sound.
▶ Next close your mouth and inhale quietly through your nose to a mental count of four.
▶ Next hold your breath for a count of seven.
▶ Then exhale completely through your mouth, making a whoosh sound to a count of eight.
▶ This is one breath. Now inhale again and repeat the cycle three more times for a total of four breaths."

Dr. Weil goes on to explain that this exercise becomes more and more powerful and effective with time and practice, and suggests doing it at least twice a day. He also recommends that, for your first month of practice, you not do more than four breaths at one time. Later, he says, you can extend it to eight breaths. He also instructs you not to be concerned if you get a bit light-headed at first when you try this breathing. It'll go away.

Excerpt from Andrew Weil, M.D., *Natural Health, Natural Medicine.* New York: Houghton Mifflin, 1995.

TECHNIQUE-Y THINGS

Now we've arrived at the fourth and last ring, the furthest circle out; the technique-y things. These I give you in one big heap for you to rummage through and check out what attracts you. I do this because although I believe a good argument can be made for how I prioritized the stuff I prioritized, these "technique-y things" are different. I don't believe they have a natural hierarchy. It's whatever grabs you, and it's a very individual matter.

Just keep in mind that these "technique-y things" are even more about "symptomatic" relief than anything we've talked about yet. They're like taking aspirin for the pain of the steamroller parked on your chest until you can get it off. They don't solve the problem but they can definitely come in handy, kind of like a life preserver until the rescue helicopter pulls you out of the sea. Know them well, and then enjoy them. Pick one that sounds cool and interesting to you and check it out. Try it. Read about it. Then pick another. Here we go.

Breathing Exercises

This is one of the big classics of most "stress reduction" books. They're full of different techniques and approaches. To me, the best advice of all about breathing is as follows:

Do it. Because most people are anxious to one degree or another, they do this teeny, thin, shallow breathing. This shuts down energy and vitality (we receive more of our nutrition through breath than through eating!) but people do it unconsciously because it also shuts down emotions, and most of us have all sorts of painful emotions that we don't want to feel. So we "numb out" by the thin, tiny breathing.

MORE WORDS-O'-WISDOM FROM LORI LEYDEN-RUBENSTEIN

"Diaphragmatic breathing [also] has a number of psychological effects including the capacity to increase ego strength, emotional stability, confidence, alertness and the perceived control over one's environment. It also decreases anxiety, phobic behavior, depression and psychosomatic illness."

Excerpt from Lori Leyden-Rubenstein, *The Stress Management Handbook.* **New Canaan, Conn.: Keats Publishing, 1998.**

The natural way for humans to breathe is demonstrated by babies: nice, full, free, easy breaths that move like waves through the whole rib cage and belly and back, too! This is a healthy organism. No holding at the end of the inhalation or the exhalation. Not a "controlled" or "manipulated" breath; just a free, easy, natural breath. So go ahead and experiment with breathing techniques if you want, but mostly, become aware of how you're always restricting and constricting your breath; holding it, holding back, holding up, holding on. You don't have to willfully "take deep, full breaths," though that feels great if you've been breathing shallow, but really all you have to do is stop impeding it; stop getting in the way of it; stop "clenching" around your gut, your solar plexus, your ribs. And the body will breathe deep and free on its own, in a healthy, natural way.

Deep Relaxation

Here's another big favorite of stress reduction books. There's a few zillion approaches but most of them go more or less like this: Lay down on your back or sit in a comfy chair. Close your eyes. (Pause.) Feel your breath moving in and out. (Pause.) Bring your attention to the top or bottom of your body. (Crown of head or feet.)

And very slowly imagine each part, part by part, releasing and relaxing, like: feet (pause) ankles (pause) calves and knees (pause) upper legs/thighs (pause) hips and pelvis (pause) low back and stomach . . . you get the idea. Some systems have you actually tense the muscles of each area for a few seconds and then release. Others have you imagine a warm energy moving through, releasing and relaxing each part as you go. Some just have you tune into your body and gently scan through with your awareness, finding places that are "holding on," then you "invite" that part to release, to soften, to let go. Other approaches "count you down" like in hypnosis, envisioning yourself descending down, down, down, deeper, deeper, deeper somehow (a diving bell in the sea or whatever you like). Some have you imagine yourself very heavy, some light as a feather.

There are countless approaches and you can get all sorts of books, tapes, and CDs and so on. If you have Internet access, go onto somewhere like amazon.com and punch in stress, stress reduction, relaxation, stuff like that. You can also make your own tape. Speak in a slow, relaxed, calming voice, leaving a lot of silent space.

This guided relaxation is something you get better at with practice, so you have to give it a good chance if it seems interesting to you.

Meditation

This is another colossal one, a veritable monster in the "stress reduction" arsenal. In the spiritual traditions they were looted from, meditation was and is a much more profound matter than mere "stress reduction" but since this is a book about stress reduction (relaxation creation) here's what you should know: Basically, all meditation techniques work with and train your attention. Mostly they just vary in what "object" of attention they use. The most common "objects of attention" in stress-reduction versions of meditation are the breath or a mantra, which is a made-up sound or word repeated silently in your mind. Sometimes a candle flame is used. Other approaches have you simply sit quietly and observe your passing thoughts like clouds in the sky, without getting caught up in them. Probably the premier stress reduction meditation system is Transcendental Meditation, or TM.

People are typically instructed to meditate anywhere from 15 minutes to 30 minutes, twice a day. No matter what kind of meditation you do, most systems emphasize not getting frustrated when your attention wanders and you get caught up thinking about how the Lakers are doing in the Finals, or about a big date coming up, or about your lack of any big date coming up. This kind of thing happens constantly for all novice meditators. Just gently, compassionately, and persistently bring your attention back to your "object" again, (breath, mantra, etc.). And again. And again. With great patience.

TM

TM, short for Transcendental Meditation, is probably the most popularly well-known technique of relaxation-oriented meditation in the world. Five million people worldwide practice TM, and the effectiveness of the Transcendental Meditation program has been validated by over 500 scientific studies at more than 200 independent research institutions in 30 countries. To quote their Web site (www.tm.org): "A statistical meta-analysis conducted at Stanford University of all available studies—146 independent outcomes—indicated that the effect of the TM program on reducing anxiety as a character trait was much greater than that of all other meditation and relaxation techniques, including muscle relaxation."

Affirmation & Creative Visualization

The basic idea here is that since your experience of events is determined by your thinking, you try to alter your habitual thought habits and "tape loops" by planting positive, healthy, desirable thoughts and beliefs and images in your mind. Once again, there are countless systems, approaches, methods and books. The classic is still probably Shakti Gawain's *Creative Visualization*. Many of them combine the guided relaxation stuff, so you do the guided relaxation, and then while you're laying there all deeply relaxed and receptive, you start saying your affirmations silently to yourself. Or you put the whole shebang—the guided relaxation and the affirmations—on a tape and do it that way. Some examples of affirmations for us stress-prone people are:

"I am now deeply relaxed and at ease."
"I am letting go and trusting life."

There are other systems that have you write them over and over again, like, say, for 15 minutes every morning and 15 minutes every night. It's sort of like reprogramming the software of your mind.

Go ahead and write your own customized, tailor-made affirmations of your own. Key points are these:

1. Make sure you state what you want in positive terms ("I am serene, tranquil, at peace.") and *never* in negative terms ("I am no longer stressed-out. My tension is vanishing.").

2. You must state what you want in present tense, present terms, as if what you want is already the case. So you never say, "I *will be* light, loose, and carefree." You say, "I *am* light, loose, and carefree."

3. Keep them short and simple.

4. You have to persevere; regularity is the key. Stick with the same several affirmations for an extended period of time, a few weeks at least.

In her book, *The Stress Management Handbook,* Lori Leyden-Rubenstein cites research showing the following benefits from meditation:

"Clearer thinking
Less jittery
Decreased sense of urgency
Increased energy, productivity, efficiency
Decrease in anxiety
Easier to get along with
Less irritable
Less critical of self and others
Less influenced by others
Decreased feelings of pressure
More open emotionally
Less defensive
Decrease in mild depression
More self-aware
Stronger sense of inner strength/ internal validation"

Excerpt from Lori Leyden-Rubenstein, *The Stress Management Handbook.* New Canaan, Conn.: Keats Publishing, 1998.

Creative visualization is essentially the same thing but instead of using words, you use imagery of yourself. Once again you get yourself into a deeply relaxed state of mind, but now you visualize yourself going about your day in a relaxed, tranquil mood. You make it like a movie in your mind. It's important, though, during your "mental movie" to also recreate (or pre-create) other sensations too, so it's not purely visual. So, as you see yourself calm and carefree, try also to create the emotional feeling of that state of mind. Imagine bodily sensations; full, easy breaths, shoulders dropped and soft. Feel your forehead soft and smooth, make it as rich a mental movie as you can. If you do this regularly, it can become remarkably effective.

Bodywork

This means going and getting a session of massage or cranial sacral therapy or Rolfing or Trager or any of the other zillion systems of bodywork. Here, of course, we run into the issue of money. Bodywork costs money. Teenagers oftentimes don't have much of it. Plus, the relaxation that bodywork gives you is almost always quite temporary. As in a couple hours. If you have limited bucks, I would suggest putting it into therapy (see page 11–13) or even into buying a lot of the books mentioned in this book; things that address the *causes* of your stress.

Now, all that said, if you do have the spare dinero (dollars), bodywork can do two important things for the stress-ravaged.

1. It can break the stress feedback loop. The "stress feedback loop" is where you're so anxious that you're driven to do a bunch of frantic stuff and doing all that frantic stuff in turn makes you more anxious (and feeling like your

"Practice . . . meditation in the morning or in the evening or at any leisure time during the day. You will soon realize that your mental burdens are dropping away one by one, and that you are gaining an intuitive power that you could not have previously dreamed possible."

"There have been thousands upon thousands of people who have practiced meditation and obtained its fruits. Don't doubt its possibilities because of the simplicity of its method. If you can't find the truth right where you are, where else do you think you will find it?"

—The Great Zen Master Dogen, 1200–1153 B.C.

ROLFING

Rolfing is the grandmother of almost every well-known, modern sort of tissue bodywork system out there. Rolfing was developed by a scientist named Dr. Ida Rolf in the 1950s. It's a system of lengthening, freeing, and rebalancing the fascial sheaths (fascia is the connective tissue that wraps every muscle, bone, and organ in the body) and the muscles in the body to create structural alignment and integration. It is deep and powerful work, with an extraordinary and enduring reputation for overall physical improvement, pain relief, and even psychological change. But again, for our purposes, the pertinent point here is that Rolfing is astoundingly relaxing and rejuvenating.

Did you know? Trager bodywork is a gentle system that uses mindful manipulations, stretches, rocking, oscillations and other artful techniques to access the body's nervous system and holding patterns, allowing the body to release and unwind its dysfunctional patterns (tension, torsion, etc.).

day/life is hurling by, out of control). Then that increased anxiety drives you to do still more frantic stuff which in turn makes you more anxious. In other words, your own freaked-out state freaks you out, and it keeps accelerating. A good bodywork session, especially Rolfing, Trager, or craniosacral work, will turn down (way down) your sympathetic nervous system ("fight or flight" stress response) and turn on your parasympathetic nervous system (relaxation response) breaking the loop, giving you some breathing space in which to get centered again and take stock of things.

2. The deep, deep relaxation of an excellent bodywork session can be so powerful that it simply recalibrates your whole internal sense of what's possible in terms of relaxation. It can give you a new "true north" on your compass, a new sense of just how at ease and loose you can truly be. Many stressed-out people don't really know how stressed-out they are—they think it's normal. It's not. Bodywork can help you really get that.

CRANIOSACRAL WORK

Craniosacral work is an elegant and subtle form of bodywork mostly involving gentle, refined adjustments of the cranial bones (in the head) and the sacrum (base of the spine), and also involving the slow, subtle rhythm of the craniosacral pulse as it moves the cerebrospinal fluid through the spine and cranium. In the work you lay on a table, with clothes on, and the craniosacral therapist uses highly trained hands to feel aberrations, "stuck" points, and other dysfunctions throughout this craniosacral system. By restoring balance and health to the whole system, the therapist supports deep balance and healing at the level of the central nervous system. It is subtle, quiet, gentle work, but it feels terrific and is amazingly relaxing. By the way, craniosacral work also heals all sorts of actual health problems, but that discussion is outside the scope of this book.

Herbs

I myself am not a big supporter of herbs for relaxation. Using herbs seems to go nowhere near the causes of our stress. And in terms of the two reasons I gave for bodywork (break the stress loop and provide a new experience of just how much relaxation is possible for you), herbs don't, in my experience, relax you enough to do either one. But that's just me. I'm sure there are a zillion gifted herbalists out there who would argue otherwise. Just for the record, valerian and St. John's wort are two relaxing herbs that many people swear by. I simply feel that herbs absolve the user of responsibility even more than most other relaxation methods. It's the same popular mentality of, "Pop a pill," except it's herbal. Not my cup of tea, that's all.

Three Cute Little Ideas

Cute Little Idea #1: Write it down!

Write down everything and anything that's causing your stress. List the things. Journal about them. Whatever works for you. But just getting them out of the spinning circus in your head and nailed down in clear, concrete specifics, right in front of you—pinned down in black and white—can give real feelings of relief, and of being in control. People in starchy white lab-coats have done real live research on this. It truly helps.

THREE CUTE LITTLE IDEAS

▶ Write it down!
▶ Determine what you can change.
▶ Answer, what's the worst that can happen?

Cute Little Idea #2: Determine what you can change.

Then you can do something else that can help you even more. You go through and write, on your list, those things you can do something about and those things you can't do anything about. Of the things you can do stuff about, you should also write down what those actions are and when they can be done (maybe you're stressed-out about an up-coming quiz at school, but your teacher hasn't yet given out the material that the quiz will cover. So, as of now, there's nothing you can do about that quiz).

What you're doing is making an actual, real-life diagram of the AA Serenity Prayer, "God, grant me the wisdom to accept the things I cannot change, the courage to change the things I can, and the wisdom to know the difference." It's good to be able to look at all the things that are stressing you out and to see clearly, right before your blinking eyes, which things you simply can't do anything about and which things you can.

Of the things you *can* do something about (both now and later) it's even better if, on your list, you break them down into the list of very small tasks. So instead of just "study for test," you'd break it down into something like this:

1. Go to library and get resources.

2. Go on Internet and download articles.

3. Read through with highlighter, marking key points.

4. Read through half of the assigned chapter, marking important points with highlighter.

5. Read through the other half of the assigned chapter, marking important points with highlighter.

6. Read through key points and make notes about them.

7. Memorize the stuff that seems important.

Cute Little Idea #3: Answer, what's the worst that can happen?

With this one, you take the gnarly things that are threatening and pressuring you and you write down the worst-case scenarios. So you say to yourself, "Okay, I'm stressed-out by this big test. What'll happen if I fail it?" Then you answer. Maybe you say, "I'll have a lousy GPA. Maybe I won't even pass my grade." Then you go, "So then what'll happen?" and again you answer, "My parents will be bummed out and angry and give me such-and-such consequences. And maybe I'll have to go to summer school or repeat the grade. Or I won't be able to get into college." So then what will happen? And so on. You carry it out as far as you can.

And unless you're being silly and melodramatic, you basically arrive at the fact that life goes on. And it keeps changing form and changing shape and when one door closes another opens. And out of the ashes of destruction and failure come new impulses, new directions, new possibilities. There's an old joke that goes: "How do you make God laugh? Tell Him your plans."

Ultimately you find out that it's not that the "detours" are taking you out of your big life plan, but rather, that the detours *are* your life; that our lives are made up of detours, the unforeseen, the serendipities.

You notice that every situation turns out *some* way, and that life never stops moving. Energy keeps changing form and shape. You learn that nobody's life goes according to their tidy little plans, but that, for the most part, we're out of control here, and the way to be wise, creative, happy and healthy is to relax and trust and stay open and curious. A great spiritual master, Avatar Adi Da Samraj says humorously,

> *"Relax, nothing is under control."*

You learn that, just as we talked about earlier, your happiness and good feeling lie within you, not in any circumstances "out there." So no matter what situation you end up in, you can be curious, open, interested and alive in the middle of it.

So if you're grounded for a whole summer, maybe you end up using all that solitude to do some incredible reading that turns you in new directions or plants incredible new seeds. If you have to go to summer school, maybe you meet some great friends there and you also really receive and digest certain lessons about why you failed the class—procrastination, perfectionism, whatever, and those lessons serve you powerfully in the years ahead. If you can't get into college, you take a couple years gaining life experience, living, growing, learning, and maturing. Maybe you travel. Work on yourself in therapy. You take some extension courses at a small community college. And maybe along the way, a different livelihood and passion takes you off in a new direction that doesn't even require college. Or maybe you just get involved in college later, gaining entrance because of the courses you took at the small community college.

These obviously are just a small sampling of the infinite possibilities, all totally unforeseeable, that people's lives can and do take. It's a huge, wild, inconceivable, ever-changing, ever-fluid play, and there's just no possible way to judge events as "good" or "bad." Many people have even ended up feeling tremendous gratitude for life-threatening illnesses like cancer or multiple sclerosis, because it woke them up, opened their hearts, made them fall in love with life and people. You just can't judge. You just can't know. So trust. Surrender. Relax. Create radiant inner peace within yourself, a little more each day, as a gift of deep love for yourself and all your friends and this planet of ours.

Summary

There you have it, folks, everything you need to begin your adventure into creating ease and relaxation. Ultimately, creating relaxation and serenity is the greatest journey there is in life. Because to truly get rid of stress involves tremendous bravery: facing your insecurities, your fear, and your anger. To truly, creatively address your stress is to face yourself, a courageous way of living, which very few people in this world choose.

So begin the endless exploration of the center of the bull's eye, simultaneously work with the first ring out, and whenever you feel like it, artfully, creatively play around with the second, third, and fourth rings. Let this book and others be your springboard from which you begin the amazing odyssey to a peaceful, easy, loose, expansive way of being. Take hold of this process. Get into it. Make it your own. May you enjoy each and every step on the path into deep and radiant inner peace.

Ultimately creating relaxation and serenity is the greatest journey there is in life.

Resources

BOOK RESOURCES

Adi Da Samraj. *What, Where, When, How, Why and Who to Remember to Be Happy*. Middletown, Calif.: Dawn Horse Press, 2000.
Beautifully illustrated children's book teaching essential, mind-stopping Spiritual Truths. Don't let the fact that this simple, happy, playful book is a children's book fool you: its communication is shiny and profound and penetrating for teenagers and adults, too.

Banks, Syd. *Second Chance*. Tampa, Fla.: Duval-Bibb Publishing Company, 1990.
This is the story of a stressed-out, miserable businessman who had a simple but profound shift or awakening into a new peaceful way of being in the world. Very "quick read" and very accessible, but inspiring. Syd Banks and his teaching were the catalyst for the Psychology of Mind (mentioned many times throughout this book) approach to mental health and happiness.

Beattie, Melodie. *Codependent No More*. Center City, Minn.: Hazelden Information Education, 1996.
For a great many people, one of the most stressful things in life is codependency, the compulsive drive to fix, control or worry about others while neglecting self-care. This book is one of the classics in the codependency field.

Benson, Herbert, M.D. *The Relaxation Response*. New York: Morrow/Avon, 2000.
The original classic (revised in 2000) on all the science showing how dramatically Transcendental Meditation® creates relaxation in the body and mind.

Bradshaw, John. *Healing the Shame That Binds You*. Deerfield Beach, Fla.: Health Communications, 1988.
John Bradshaw is extremely well known and well respected in the fields of family therapy and recovery. A basic understanding of shame, what it is and how it functions in us should be required reading for nearly everyone.

Brother Lawrence. *The Practice of the Presence of God*. Springdale, Pa.: Whitaker House, 1982.
For those moved toward exploring spirituality in a Christian vein. This is a beautiful, humble, wise, easily understandable little book, written about 300 years ago.

Carlson, Richard, and Joseph Bailey. *Slowing Down to the Speed of Life*. San Francisco: HarperSanFrancisco, 1997.
This is a highly readable book by two Psychology of Mind practitioners. It provides an easily understandable explanation of how our busy, stressed-out experience of life derives from our own thinking, not from "the world out there." Richard Carlson's book, *Don't Sweat the Small Stuff . . . and it's all small stuff* is also a simple and exceptional little book.

Chodron, Pema. *Start Where You Are*. Boston: Shambala, 2001.
Pema Chodron is an extremely popular Tibetan Buddhist teacher and was a student of Chogyam Trungpa. This book is highly regarded, especially its ideas on stress and life in general.

Dass, Ram. *Journey of Awakening*. New York: Bantam Books, 1990 (rev.).
An excellent sort of general, overall guidebook for people interested in meditation. Ram Dass is a classic, well-regarded Eastern philosophy dude who has been "on the scene" for over 30 years. His classic 1971 book, *Be Here Now* (Crown Publishers) is also definitely worth a read.

Davis, Martha, et al. *The Relaxation and Stress Reduction Workbook*. Oakland, Calif.: New Harbinger Publications, 2000.

Somatics Magazine calls this book, "the bible on stress reduction." If you're interested in *techniques* for stress reduction, this is the one for you. It is densely packed full of techniques, instructions, and exercises.

Emmett, Rita. *The Procrastinator's Handbook*. New York: Walker & Company, 2000.

There are zillions of books on procrastination. This one is simple, direct, practical and full of wonderful little tidbits of wisdom. I heartily recommend this book . . . eminently useable.

Hanh, Thich Nhat. Anything by Thich Nhat Hanh.

This beautiful and peaceful Zen monk writes clear, simple nutritious books in a straightforward, easy-to-understand way. Two of his books are *Peace is Every Step* and *Being Peace*.

Hoff, Benjamin. *The Tao of Pooh*. New York: Penguin Putnam Incorporated, 1983.

As amazon.com tells us, "Romp through the enchanting world of Winnie-the-Pooh while soaking up invaluable lessons on simplicity and natural living." A fun, playful, but still profound look at Taoism through the spectrum of Winnie-the-Pooh characters. A classic and a favorite of many.

Huber, Cheri. Anything by her! (Keep it Simple Books.)

Cheri Huber gives us a blend of unobtrusive Zen Buddhism mixed with deeply compassionate, humanistic psychology, but she does it in an amazingly gentle, simple, living, nurturing way. Her books are very easy and very healing to read. If you only check out one resource from this booklist, check out Cheri Huber. I recommend *any* of her books, but if I had to pick a few, I'd go with: *There Is Nothing Wrong with You*, *The Key*, or *The Fear Book*.

Jampolsky, Gerald G. *Love Is Letting Go of Fear*. Berkeley, Calif.: Celestial Arts, 1995.

Another clear, simple, pristine and loving communication, cultivating kindness and tenderness toward others and ourselves. This same author has a wonderful book about guilt, too.

Kurtz, Ernest, and Katherine Ketchum. *The Spirituality of Imperfection*. New York: Bantam Books, 1992.
This is a tremendous book. It's not particularly geared toward teenagers, but I think any teenager interested in spirituality would really get a lot out of this sane, wise, thoughtful book. If I had to sum up its essence, I'd say it's this: Our spirituality blossoms when we fully accept and embrace our woundedness and imperfection.

Lao-tzu. *Tao Te Ching*. Translated by Stephen Mitchell. New York: Harper & Row, 1988.
The *Tao Te Ching* (pronounced "dow day jing") is the most widely translated book in the world after the Bible. This ancient and amazing wisdom, communicated in semi-poetic stanzas, is like healing nectar for the stressed-out. It conveys (among other things) the deep serenity and sanity of a life-attitude of *being* rather than *doing*.

Needleman, Jacob. *Time and the Soul*. New York: Currency/Doubleday, 1998.
A richly contemplative and eloquently written book on the roots of our experience of time scarcity. Philosophical and thought provoking.

Robbins, John. *Diet For A New World*. New York: Avon Books, 1992.
Read this book. That's all I can say. Read it. Exceptional, required reading for any and all humans. And then continue with his books, *The Food Revolution* and *Diet for a New America*. These books will change your health, your life and the planet. Check 'em out, and I don't mean maybe.

Sark. Anything by Sark. Wonderful books about being kind to yourself, taking pleasure in life, having fun, accepting, trusting, and being who you are, creating and loving life. These are simple, buoyant, juicy, rich, happy books. Fun and giggles to read, and nurturing to the soul. Highly recommended! Two great ones to start with are *The Bo-*

dacious Book of Succulence: Daring to Live Your Succulent Wild Life or *Transformation Soup: Healing for the Splendidly Imperfect* (both from Fireside Publications).

Schaef, Anne Wilson. *Meditations for Living in Balance: Daily Solutions for People Who Do Too Much*. San Francisco: SanFranciscoHarper, 2000.

Anne Wilson Schaef is a major "shaker and mover" in the addictions recovery world. This book, and her book, *Meditations for Women Who Do Too Much* (excellent for men, too), are excellent little source-books full of tremendously helpful reflections, tidbits and slices of wisdom to absorb into our being. Highly recommended.

Trungpa, Chogyam. *Shambala: Sacred Path of the Warrior*. Boston: Shambala, 1995.

This is a wonderful, nonreligious presentation of Tibetan Buddhist technique, philosophy and psychology discussed in terms of universal principles such as fearlessness, compassion and so on. It's a fairly in-depth book (i.e., not a "quick read") but very rich and deeply intelligent. Chogyam Trungpa was a great and extremely well-respected Tibetan Buddhist Master of the highest order.

Watts, Alan. *The Wisdom of Insecurity*. New York: Vintage Books, 1968.

Alan Watts is another very big deal, classic Eastern philosophy guy, especially popular in the 1960s and 1970s. He played a gigantic role in popularizing Zen (and Eastern philosophy in general) in the West. You could do well with pretty much any of his writings, but this book is particularly relevant to people who want a more profound, spiritual and/or philosophical dimension to dealing with stress.

Wilde, Stuart. *Life Was Never Meant to Be a Struggle*. Carlsbad, Calif.: Hay House, 1998.

I love this guy! Stuart Wilde is an eccentric, a power-house, a character, and a profound, rollicking, flamboyant and funny guy with a feisty, charismatic and mischievous attitude. This is a teensy little book, small and thin enough to carry in your back pocket, but it's a great one.

THREE OTHER GREAT BOOKS

Carlson, Richard. *Don't Sweat the Small Stuff . . . and it's all small stuff: Simple Ways to Keep the Little Things from Taking Over Your Life.* New York: Hyperion, 1997.

St. James, Elaine. *Inner Simplicity: 100 Ways to Regain Peace and Nourish Your Soul.* New York: Hyperion, 1995.

Suzuki, Shunryu. *Zen Mind, Beginner's Mind: Informal Talks on Zen Meditation and Practice.* New York: Weatherhill, 1970 (version: 1999). This book is a great classic in Soto Zen literature.

RESOURCES FOR 12-STEP RECOVERY

www.7in1web.com/best/recovery.htm
In this one, 12-Step meetings' official Web sites are listed. Only 12-Step Web sites that are maintained by the respective organization are listed. http://12stepmeetings.org/thelist.s

Workaholics Anonymous—Support group in which members can retain anonymity presents news and a reading list. Find the group's meeting schedules in various states too. http://people.ne.mediaone.net/wa2

RESOURCES ON THE NASTINESS OF TV

Kill Your Television—Collection of essays on the evils of television including ads, effects on kids. Information on TV turnoff weeks and a bibliography. www.netreach.net/~kaufman

TV Sucks—TeVil: Television is Evil. http://w3.nai.net/~perfecto/tevil.html

"Evils of Imagery—Some People Think Images are Evil!" Neil Postman, in his book *Amusing Ourselves to Death,* warns us of the evils of imagery. He contends that television and the age of computers have contributed to the downfall of intellectual thought. www.bignet.net/~cmel/evilimagery.html

A FEW GOOD DIET RESOURCES

Dr. Gabriel Cousens—Web site sponsored by Dr. Gabriel Cousens. Dr. Gabriel Cousens is the founder of the Tree of Life organization and retreat based in Patagonia, Arizona. www.rawfood.com/cousens.html

Conscious Eating—*Conscious Eating* by Gabriel Cousens, M.D., Essene Vision Books, 1996, 558 pages. Available in paperback only. Perhaps the most influential book on live foods to date. www.vegan.com/bookstore/all_books/446

EarthSave International—Group advocates a plant-based, earth-friendly diet. Meet founder and author John Robbins, read news stories and learn about local chapters. www.earthsave.org

The Food Revolution—Definitely check this one out! The Food Revolution reveals the truth about popular diets, genetically modified foods, mad cow disease, and the health effects of what you eat in this long-awaited and provocative book and accompanying Web site. www.foodrevolution.org

THERAPIST REFERRAL RESOURCES

1-800-THERAPIST—Extensive referral network and international therapist marketing service offers help in choosing a counselor and provides news and related links. www.1-800-therapist.com www.therapy-referral.com www.therapistreferral.com www.find-a-therapist.com

PSYCHOLOGY OF MIND RESOURCES

www.psychologyofmind.com 1-800-481-7639 (US), 1-541-383-9362 (Intl.)
www.philosophyofliving.com
Personal telephone and e-counseling services: US Allan Flood 1-541-389-9781

TRANSCENDENTAL MEDITATION

www.TM.org

Index

About the Author and Illustrator

Mark Powell teaches physical education, creative writing, English, and martial arts at a Waldorf-inspired high school. He has taught at the school for over 13 years. Powell is also a certified Rolfer, nutritional consultant, writer, spiritual practitioner, and a recovering stressed-out guy. He lives with his wife in Minneapolis, Minnesota.

Kelly Adams has been known to many in the resort town of Vail, Colorado, as a "child prodigy." At the age of eighteen months, she was already drawing clear pictures of animals. Her first art show was in Vail at age six. Kelly's art has been prominently displayed throughout town on busses, in brochures, in public libraries, and other numerous showings of drawings and sculptures. She has won many awards including two years of DaVinci Awards, the Advanced Art Achievement Award, and the 1997 and 1998 Peace Poster Awards for the Lion's Club at the state level. In the future she plans to attend art college and write and create her own comic books.